REFLECTION AND ACTION

PHAENOMENOLOGICA

COLLECTION FONDÉE PAR H.L. VAN BREDA ET PUBLIÉE
SOUS LE PATRONAGE DES CENTRES D'ARCHIVES-HUSSERL

97

REFLECTION AND ACTION

NATHAN ROTENSTREICH

REFLECTION AND ACTION

NATHAN ROTENSTREICH

1985 **MARTINUS NIJHOFF PUBLISHERS**
a member of the KLUWER ACADEMIC PUBLISHERS GROUP
DORDRECHT / BOSTON / LANCASTER

B
105
.A35
R67
1985

Distributors

for the United States and Canada: Kluwer Academic Publishers, 190 Old Derby Street, Hingham, MA 02043, USA
for the UK and Ireland: Kluwer Academic Publishers, MTP Press Limited, Falcon House, Queen Square, Lancaster LA1 1RN, UK
for all other countries: Kluwer Academic Publishers Group, Distribution Center, P.O. Box 322, 3300 AH Dordrecht, The Netherlands

Library of Congress Cataloging in Publication Data

Rotenstreich, Nathan, 1914–
  Reflection and action.

  (Phaenomenologica ; 97)
  1. Act (Philosophy) I. Title. II. Series.
B105.A35R67 1984   128'.4   84-6066
ISBN 90-247-2969-6

ISBN 90-247-2969-6 (this volume)
ISBN 90-247-2339-6 (series)

Copyright

© 1985 by Martinus Nijhoff Publishers, Dordrecht.

PRINTED IN THE NETHERLANDS

CONTENTS

AUTHOR'S NOTE

The present analysis is meant to be of phenomenological character. It explores the conditions for action as an intervention in the world and as an establishment of structures aside the given reality. It deals with these conditions both in terms of human attitude — reflection — and in terms of the nature of reality — its openness. No attempt is made to exhaust all the directions of activity. Those selected are considered either as basic or as exhibiting some singular traits.

The phenomenological character of the analysis is not designed to follow a doctrine or school. It is rather meant to adhere to a certain method, namely to understand structures, as it were, from within. Yet this character of the analysis calls for an attempt to learn from the exploration of action in different philosophical trends. We must mention, in addition to the references in the text, the concern with action in various contemporary analytic writings. Pragmatism is obviously instructive, as are the works of Stuart Hampshire, Thomas Morawetz, Jürgen Habermas and Richard Bernstein.

I am grateful to Ms. M. Reich for the finishing touches she gave to the text.

N.R.
Jerusalem 1983

CHAPTER ONE

ATTITUDE AND HORIZON

(1)

The subject of the present analysis is action and activity in several of their configurations. In each of the configurations that we shall analyze, we shall discern the inherent component of a reflective attitude. It is also suggested that actions and activities have some structure and built-in rules, which are accepted, tacitly or saliently, implicitly or explicitly, once one is engaged in a certain line of activity. Hence it is apposite as a kind of preamble to the analysis of types of activities to give some attention to the attitude and phenomenon of reflection, or, to put it as a pun — an outcome of the phenomenon itself — to reflect upon reflection.

(2)

It is well known that the term 'reflection' derives from the optical sphere. In a broader sense it connotes an attitude of bending back. But once we retreat or bend back, we turn our attention or our thoughts to our own thinking. In this context, and this, too, is well known, reflection amounts to turning one's thoughts or attention to (a) the act of thinking, (b) the content of our thinking, (c) the validity of our thought. Thus reflection itself is a configuration or a structure of these components, with all the aspects of interaction or correlation that go with it. In thinking, for instance, to use two German expressions which are pertinent for the description or phenomenological analysis of reflection, we may first consider *Überlegung*, where the emphasis would lie on the *über*; that is to say, in a sense, that in reflecting we are positing ourselves above the acts and the thoughts, both in their substantive connotation and in their intentionality towards validity. We are thrown back, but by the same token we elevate ourselves, as it were, above the primary situation. The second German expression, *Nachdenken*, with its emphasis on the *nach*, has a temporal connotation, that is to say, in an act of reflection we follow a previous situation, be it what it may, but we also think over that situation, give it additional attention, etc. The two expressions are in a sense interrelated, since in order to be above a situation, we have to come back to it, and the very coming back is already a step from the first retreat to the focus of our, as it were, second coming. To sum up this preliminary description, we would say that we are referring to the positional aspect of reflection. Our activities and our thinking go on in their usual flow, but concurrently we 'overlook' and 'look back' on that flow.

(3)

We may ask at this point whether or not there are certain stimuli, to use the common expression, for the activity of looking back, overlooking, etc. The two stimuli which can be identified in the first place, at least on the day-to-day level of existence, are the activities of correcting our previous thinking, carrying out our plans, and the parallel aspect of planning new activities or formulating new thoughts. The aspect of stepping back is indeed very visible in acts of correction, since the attitude of correcting is by definition related to something we have already done or brought about. Doing, in this broad sense, comprises our own thinking, and not only our intervention in the course of events, like our activity of engaging in certain pursuits and negotiations, but also in outcomes which are interpreted not as achievements, but as failures. Reflection is involved in corrections in the sense that we read the situation as it is, and plan or decide to intervene in it in order to change its course or outcome. In this sense, correction is already a kind of planning, because we entertain in our thinking that which we want or have wanted to achieve, compare it with the existing state of affairs and map out an activity which will lead to a different result or outcome. The last aspect can be identified as planning, even in a very limited sense. To be sure, planning is not necessarily intertwined with turning our thought to that which has been done; it is a broader orientation referring to the future. As such, the future may comprise within its scope the to-be-attained outcome of our activity which will also correct the past. The future is not only a locus of devices for the sake of the past, but is obviously also the dimension of what is about to occur. In our plannings we take into account the broad dimension of the future as the locus of occurrences to be. In focusing on planning, we focus on that which we are about to do in order to bring about certain occurrences in the future. Here we can discern the attitude of turning our thought *qua* reflection in the limited sense of the term, because we entertain in our thinking the dimension of the future as a dimension of time. We read the meaning of that dimension or interpret it in terms of its openness to the events or occurrences which are due to take place and have not yet taken place. Finally, we concentrate on directing ourselves in bringing about those occurrences which we plan to bring about. In this sense, reflection is an essential ingredient of the attitude and activity of planning and can be described in a term parallel to that of *Nachdenken — Vordenken*.

(4)

The last component of the reflective attitude can be identified as that of anticipation. The turning of the thought amounts here to anticipating the content of time *qua* future. We started with a description of the positional aspect of reflection because of the element of stepping back present in it; now we can very early identify in our analysis of reflection both the position and an aspect of the content. At this juncture, it is the position in time of the content, i.e. the future.

Here we also notice a symmetry or correlation in terms of the position in time of the two directions of the reflective activity with which we started our analysis: in correcting — with all its variations — we turn towards the past; in planning and anticipating we turn towards the future. To be sure, the expected result of our corrective activity anticipates the result, and thus we entertain at the same time the direction towards the past and the direction towards the future. In this sense the foci of reflection are time-oriented in terms of the dimensions of time, but the reflective attitude as such is, as it were, above time, because it wavers between the two dimensions and is literally *Überlegung*. Because of the latter element inherent in reflection, we can say that in what we metaphorically described as stepping back, we already notice a distance between reflection and the situation or state of affairs referred to. That distance is enhanced by the bifocal direction of reflection toward the past and toward the future. In other words, reflection is not bound by the state of affairs it reflects upon, nor by the locus of the state of affairs. Reflection itself creates its distance and overcomes it, as it were, by its intentionality towards the state of affairs, which is its focus or subject matter. The same act or configuration carries in itself, therefore, both the attitude of self-distantiation and approximation towards the state of affairs *vis-à-vis* which we took our attitude of distantiation. Reflection, therefore, appears in this context as a multi-faceted attitude or activity.

We can sum up this part of our analysis by indicating not the stimulus for reflection but its function. Since we started with the corrective and anticipating-planning aspects of reflection, we may present this line of orientation of reflection as instrumental: reflection here serves an objective of correcting or planning, and it is activized because of these objectives. In a broader sense — and this is obviously significant for the various spheres of action — we may refer here to the teleological aspect of reflection. To be sure, we do not insist on the instrumental genesis of reflection, because the primary component of stepping back in its various nuances is presupposed when we deal with the instrumental aspects of reflection. The stimuli give a direction to that presupposed activity of reflection, concentrating it on the objectives related to past performance or to the anticipated future.

We have already introduced the notion of concentration, to which we shall now give some additional attention.

(5)

Concentration has a primary connotation in terms of a physical fixing and that connotation is parallel to that of reflection. Certainly, we now use the term in the sense of directing our attention to a certain object, theme or situation. What is significant for the understanding of the impact of concentration on the nature and trend of reflection is that concentration does not occur automatically. It differs, for instance, from experience, once we take experience as connoting a condition of being affected or undergoing a certain exposure to impressions. Concentration does not start with the subject matter, but with reflection, namely with giving attention, and thus separating the issue attended to from the flow of impressions. There emerges here a correlation between ourselves concentrating on a certain theme, and the theme which is brought into prominence and in a way becomes isolated from the surroundings, precisely because concentration is directed to it. Hence, in a way, concentration gives rise to what can be described as a centre of reflection; in this sense the centre of reflection, on the thematic end, is parallel to concentration on the attitudinal one. This can be put differently by saying that concentration introduces into the stream of impressions and experiences an element of stability, precisely because the focus is now on a certain issue, theme or situation. We may come to the conclusion that the issue at stake is stable or permanent, as, for instance, the stability of certain events or their recurring pattern like dawn and dark. But these events and their structures become subject matters of our awareness only when we focus our awareness on them. The situational stability or the permanence of objects becomes a feature of the thematic sphere once the isolating and discerning character of concentration is activized. Concentration does not create the situation but brings it into prominence, even when the act of bringing into prominence discerns thematic aspects in the situation which corroborate the reflective character of concentration. In this sense, there is a primacy of concentration — indeed, not as a constitutive intentionality, but as a discerning one.

At this point we may emphasize the distinguishing character of reflection and concentration, for instance, the ability to make distinctions between the permanent or more lasting element in the theme or situation, and the fleeting elements — those which disappear. This distinction between the permanent and the disappearing elements becomes a central issue in our various attempts to realize situations or themes in their structure, either to recognize impressions or to attempt to go beyond them. Speaking of distinctions, we do not confine our analysis to the elements within a theme or topic, since the distinctions between topics, the very identification of one object versus another — all these are manifestations of the reflective activity and its concentrating hard core. In the previous part of our analysis, we emphasized the instrumental or teleological aspect of reflection since we started off with the activity of correcting and anticipating. It is clear now that correction and anticipation presuppose concentration, though in these attitudes concentration takes the character of leading to a certain intervention in the course of events or actions, while initially it has a — or only — component of observing and not interfering.

At this point we already realize the complexity of interactions between the intervening attitude and the observing one. We started with the intervening attitude because it appears on the horizon of our behaviour as a primary attitude. But even when we are not conscious of the concentration which is inherent in intervention, an analysis of its elements and presuppositions leads us to the identification of the impact of concentration and its presence. Moreover, we realize the spectrum of expressions of reflection: in one sense reflection is present or implied in the corrective and the anticipatory positions, and *pari passu* reflection is a precondition of those positions. Hence, we can sum up by saying that the result of our exploration is that reflection appears in its two-fold character: (a) as an element present in different attitudes and (b) as an attitude of its own. There is indeed a line of continuity from presentness to precondition. Yet the identification of the position of precondition calls for a more elaborate reflection on reflection, that is to say, for an identifying separation of reflection from its involvement in other attitudes, which may be primary in the sense of day-to-day existence or even awareness, but are not primary in terms of the architectonic structure of reflection.

(6)

Concentration amounts —at least from a certain point of view — to identification. We identify the subject matter and we also identify the adequate attitude towards the subject matter. If the subject matter were colours, we identify them as such, read them individually or within the spectrum of colours, organizing them in groups or classes like basic colours and others. If the subject matter is the colour to be painted, we anticipate the colour and identify the means by which the colour will be applied to the canvas. The identification implies here in the first case the attitude of what we call reading or naming, and in the second case the attitude of anticipation and intervention. Identification is not only a precondition for intervention, it also accompanies it in the process of application, for instance, whether or not the colour on the canvas meets our anticipation, fits the configuration — either that already emerging on the canvas or that conceived and planned. It goes without saying that identification is related to differentiation or distinctions, which are just the other side of the same coin. When we identify a colour as red, we at least implicitly, distinguish it from brown. A deliberate application of reflection brings about the awareness of distinctions, either as a result of our reflection, aimed at, or as a result and outcome of the act of reflection. We come, therefore, to the conclusion that the reflective attitude, along with its thematic element which implies concentration, curtails at least *post factum* the element of drawing border lines between subject matters, themes, situations, etc. Once we apply reflection deliberately, as for instance in scientific explorations or in philosophy, the various sides of the reflective approach become intentionally our subject matter. The deliberate activization of reflection amounts here to the realization of the various components of reflection, which otherwise would remain partial or latent. When we plan to draw the whole map of the attitude of reflection, we obviously make the exploration of reflection as such the subject matter of our exploration. To use Spinoza's term, the idea of the idea, the idea of the idea of the idea, etc., and the full regressive process emerge here as the structure of the very reflective intentionality once that intentionality is activized for its own sake, that is to say, once we are engaged in reflection on reflection.

(7)

We started with correction and anticipation and moved to concentration. There is a difference between the two former attitudes and the latter: the former are attitudes with a certain direction, while the latter is, in a sense, an attitude *qua* framework. It is within concentration where the directive attitudes take place, including correction and anticipation. Since we are involved in the regressive structure of reflection, we may even say that concentration, being an attitude of focusing as such, is presupposed in the directive attitudes. Within this structure we can mention also interpretation as exposition or explanation. Interpretation, as such, can be conceived as reading the meaning of a theme or of a situation, integrating the meaning in other meanings, etc. Here, again, one could say that in order to correct a state of affairs, or to anticipate it, one has to concentrate on it and interpret it. The two attitudes are analytically distinguishable. But, as a matter of fact, they coincide, since by interpreting we concentrate, and there would be no concentration, as said before, without a thematic focus; the very identification of that focus is already an interpretation. When we move a step further and ask ourselves questions like: what shall or should we do in a certain situation — the various reflective attitudes are brought together. The 'should do' contains in itself both correction and anticipation, concentration and interpretation, and in addition to that, an understanding of a meaning implied in the 'shall' or the 'should', its anticipated position, and its corrective impact on the state of affairs as it is. The 'should' can again have different meanings, according to the context in which we reflect or operate; the rule of a game, which is in a sense a norm, has a different position from the rule of justice or mercy, at least from the point of view of the comprehensiveness of the position — the rules of the game are valid only in terms of the game, while justice or mercy are valid in terms of the broad human situation. These distinctions between contexts and *pari passu* between different norms applicable to them again contain interpretation *qua* exposition of that which is encountered and that which follows from the encounter. Reflection here on the one hand refers to the norms, and on the other is vindicated by them.

If we now bring into the picture preferences, which are again modes of attitudes, we may distinguish between levels of preference: when I prefer playing to not playing, I opt not only for a certain activity of exercise, but also for certain norms, or, from the other end, they are imposed on me because they circumscribe the very sphere of the game as an activity for which I opt. When I prefer work to idleness, or rigid standards to flexibility, I interpret situations, see myself involved in them, see the consequences which follow for me and for my fellow men. I see also the relationship between the situation and the norm, since the norm is applicable not to a single situation only. Hence, the concentration and the interpretation lead us here to distinguish between the particular situation here and now, and the norm to-be-applied, which by definition is broader than the situation to which it is to be applied. In this sense interpretation embraces in itself the distinction between the singularity of the situation as an event and the breadth of the norm as a meaning which is to guide the situation and which will emerge out of the point of departure of the situation given bringing us to that which we shape by the very application of the norm. In these aspects of reflection in its various ingredients, we realize that reflection amounts to what can be described as going beyond that which is immediately given: by stepping back, we regress from that which is immediately given, and intervening in it we do the same. Eventually this rhythm applies also to the different steps we take while involved in reflection and its various nuances, tacit or salient.

(8)

It has to be observed that in these explorations and attempts to bring into prominence the various elements of reflection, we are consciously dealing with acts or attitudes. Therefore, we face the question of the congruence between these acts. One of the most prominent modes of resolving the difficulties of the congruence and safeguarding, as it were, the unity of reflection, is to suppose or presuppose a carrier, i.e. a subject of reflection or reflections, namely the 'I' or the ego. Yet when we take a look at the position of the various directions of reflection, we are bound to come to the conclusion that positing a subject *qua* 'I' is in itself a reflective act. It is an interpretation, which as such is going to meet certain problems or loopholes in the variety of the reflective acts. Because we ask the question whether reflection is permanent and realize that acts are not permanent, but that there is a stream of acts — a stream of acts of reflection, as there is a stream of experiences — we interpret that stream as belonging to, or we are grounding it in, a permanent subject. We distinguish between experiencing and reflecting and ask whether or not there is a unity behind these modes of approaching the data. Here we shift the emphasis from permanence to unity, though there exists a certain affinity of these two aspects. Again we may say that the unity is due not to the acts, but to the subject behind them or interwoven in them. Hence, the positing of the permanent or united and unifying subject is the other side of an interpretation, or, in other words, a certain response to a certain question: only when we ask about permanence or unity are we led to the act of positing the subject. In such a second-tier reflection we are moving within the sphere of acts only. To go beyond the acts is due to a certain 'focused' consideration. If this is so, then the question of the subject or the 'I' may emerge in one context of our reflective exploration, and not in another.

To refer to an example: in certain modes of action, for instance in transactions of exchangeability taking place here and now, the permanent character of the person is not a constitutive element of the process if the exchange takes place between two commodities like butter and shoes. Only when we plan for the next step in the direction of exchangeability do we presuppose that the person will be there, either as a producer or consumer or both. To be sure, roles like that of consumer or producer sound as if they refer to permanent positions of agents, of persons or of egos. But essentially they are functional descriptions and not ontological ones. They are not related by their positions to the ego as such. But when we look at another context, for instance that of accountability, responsibility, decision, etc. the position of the 'I' is of a different order: to be responsible is not to be identical with the intercourse between those engaged in situations. To be responsible amounts to a position of stepping back and, as it were, overlooking the interaction and ascribing or being called to ascribe to oneself the causative position *vis-à-vis* the action and the consequences which may, or should, follow from the acts. When we take an additional step and also introduce motivations into the context of actions, we presuppose a subject characterized by inclinations, drives, decisions, pondering, weighing, etc. Thus we introduce a second level of consideration or reflection: there emerges before our eyes a correlation between the reflective attitude and the positing of the subject or of the 'I'. That positing in turn is contextual, as is made visible by the difference between the interchangeability of producing and consuming and that between acting and being responsible or acting and being responsive.

Hence, we may sum up by saying that we start with the notion of the primacy of reflection. That notion leads us to discern different elements of reflection, different positional propositions as to the contexts of action and the various − implied or explicit − presuppositions of those contexts. From this we may move to our first step, namely that a certain conception of reality is presupposed in order to make reality accessible to actions at all. From this exploration, we shall move to an analysis of a variety of modes of action, each of them characterized by its own structure.

CHAPTER TWO

REALITY AND PRACTICABILITY

(1)

Reality is a philosophical problem because it is a total sphere. The aspect of totality turns reality into a major subject matter of philosophical reflection; problems like spheres of reality, matter, body, soul, etc. are philosophical problems because they can be conceived as secondary spheres of reality. From the point of view of cognition, or methods serving cognition, there are different channels of exploring and interpreting reality, such as the everyday orientation or scientific disciplines, e.g. physics, chemistry and biology. It can be said that the differentiation within the channels of approaching reality corresponds to different aspects or spheres of reality. In any case, knowing is a philosophical problem, not only because it is a domain in itself but also because it refers to the totality of reality which, in view of its quality as a totality, is a philosophical problem in the first place and bestows that quality on cognition as well.

Since the aspect of totality is so prominent, we are bound to ask the question: how is it possible that acts and human deeds turn out to be a philosophical concern? It is clear that acts and deeds do not occupy the same position as reality does, since acts and deeds take place within reality and thus presuppose the total sphere of reality. Acts and deeds are either interventions in reality leaving their traces in it, or they are to be viewed as changes introduced into the structure of reality by agents and thus are not governed, at least not consciously in terms of the agents, by the rules to which changes from within reality are subsumed. The partialness of deeds and acts is, to some extent, their characteristic feature. Thus they cannot be placed on the level of reality *qua* totality.

The difference between our *prima facie* approach to the realm of reality compared with the approach to the domain of acts and deeds can be put differently: reality is the sum-total of existing facts. An act or a deed can be viewed as an existing fact, but concurrently the existing fact is the product or the outcome of the act and the deed. Moreover, if we assume that an agent brings about acts and deeds with their impact on, and traces in, reality, the intention of the agent, his reference to his objective or his preference of one line of action over different lines open to him in the first place — all these are also deeds. Hence we find the multi-levelled character of deeds, though each of the levels is in itself a fact, and thus a part of the comprehensive realm of reality.

The distinction can be presented differently: within the broad sphere of facts, we can discern a segment of facts which we do not encounter at the moment of our experiencing: facts which appear and come about, and thus fill the horizon of our encounter and experience with something which did not exist as a fact a moment before. Thus light can be encountered and experienced, but lightning is an occurrence or a fact which presents itself here and now. Once our interpretation is applied to this segment of facts, we can read into the encounter and the occurrence a change or a transition from one situation to another. This indeed is the meaning of occurring which is a fact and brings about a fact — the move from darkness to light or from childhood to adolescence. These facts can be viewed as processes. But once we refer to them as changes they are not processes in the sense of a continuum in time but are imbued *ab initio* with qualities like changes, proper new stages of behaviour, etc.

The discernment of occurrences, let alone of changes, presupposes a certain aspect inasmuch as reality is concerned. Reality, as we pointed out before, is a comprehensive domain. But being comprehensive does not make it a closed domain, meaning that whatever can be in reality is a fact already contained in it. Occurrences presuppose the openness of reality, even when we assume that the open does not amount to the new, namely, that what is occurring does not change the structure of reality in terms of its inherent lawfulness. We can grant that a movement, even a change or a transition, growth etc. follows the structure of reality. Nevertheless it holds to it the very occurrence or the very existence of facts grounded in reality. But they did not previously appear as they do at present. This can be named the relative openness of reality. And indeed this feature of reality is rather significant for a systematic attempt to place human acts and deeds within and *vis-à-vis* reality.

Acts and deeds can in the first place be viewed as occurrences, and this characterization would be the minimal characteristic feature of acts and deeds. From the point of view of the broad reality, walking being an act, one's walking is just an occurrence. As such, it brings about the change in the reality, at least in one's surroundings, since before the act occurred no walking took place; it does take place now. It is not necessary at this point, and perhaps even in general, to attempt to define the phenomenological features of acts and deeds, to go into the question of what is the motivating background for the act which has taken place, whether or not there is an act of will prompting the position of the body, i.e. walking: from the point of view of the profile of the act it is sufficient to say that a change is introduced into the surrounding reality; via the impact on the surrounding reality there is *a fortiori* an impact on reality in general.

But let us contemplate two levels or spheres of change in order to indicate an additional feature of the domain of acts. An earthquake is an occurrence in reality, but also the measuring of the earthquake is an occurrence, applied to the occurrence in reality, but certainly not identical with the former. Considered as changes, both the earthquake and its measuring are changes or occurrences. But considered as acts and deeds, only the measuring is an act or a deed applied to the occurrence, thereby turning it immediately into an object. The intervention, as a change brought about through the acts, concomitantly turns the occurrence in reality into a subject matter which is not a description of the occurrence as such but a perspective of approaching the measured occurrence. From this point of view, the act or the deed of measuring introduces into reality a perspective which is not contained in the position of the occurrence as such. In this sense the act or the deed have the quality of approaching reality in spite of their being contained in it. This can be reinforced by pointing to an additional aspect: in a sense, the earthquake changes reality and so does the act of measuring it. But immediately we become aware of the difference in the modes of change: the earthquake changes the course of reality, while the measuring changes the conception of reality which, *qua* occurrence, becomes integrated into the broad domain of reality but whose impact on reality is different from the impact of the object measured. It is this aspect which brings into prominence not only the weight of the occurrences but also the fact that the act of measuring is introduced into reality from the outside. Its difference from the object re-emphasizes the difference between occurrences which are natural and those which are artificial. The act as intervention or interference has something of an artificial character and therefore we have to distinguish, within the broad sphere of changes and occurrences, between those which are brought about in the course of reality itself and those which are brought about by interventions in reality.

Acts and deeds are thus occurrences brought about by intervention. But by the same token they can be viewed as manifestations of intervention, since the concept and attitude of intervention is broader than the particular and specific act accomplished here and now. In this sense an escape from an earthquake is also an act. As such, it is a change and is therefore an intervention in the course of reality. But the difference between escaping and measuring lies in the fact that different acts are specific modes of intervention and intervention as such means access to the open reality.

In a way we are presenting here a 'metaphysical deduction' of the agent. We do not start the characterization of acts and deeds by indicating an agent who intervenes and brings about changes in reality. We start with the broad sphere of changes and discern their different levels. Since we eventually reach the readiness for intervention as well as at actual acts of intervention, we thus find room for placing the agent who now appears as the performer of changes — those changes which are not caused by the course of events in reality itself. Again, we do not presume to assess whether or not the agent is motivated

by laws different from those which govern reality. We indicate
the agent from the topological point of view as performing interventions, but we do not attempt to characterize his ontological
position. The same applies, *mutatis mutandis*, the acts of knowledge, though acts of knowledge differ from deeds proper in
that they do not change reality but only add awareness to it.
The knower is part of the reality he knows. To be sure, the
knower, belonging to reality, introduces the perspective of
knowledge into reality while the agent, through his acts and
deeds, introduces into reality their effects, impacts, implications, etc. The philosophical significance of acts and deeds is
grounded in that position peculiar to them: they change reality
though they do not emerge in a linear way from it. Hence deeds
have the quality of reality, on the one hand, and on the other
are detached from reality in the same sense as knowledge is,
in spite of the difference between the two spheres: change in
terms of perspective and change in terms of impact. Thus we
find that acts and deeds occupy some intermediate position
between reality and knowledge.

(2)

It has to be observed that the introduction into our discourse
of the notion or the position of the agent calls for a certain
caution. A bird builds a nest — this is an act or a deed — and
there is a product of the act, namely the nest. The building of
the nest by the bird differs from the existence of the bird in
the context of reality in which the bird is implicated. Hence, if
we introduce, at this point, the concept of the agent, we have
to distinguish between an agent in the general sense and the
agent as the person in the various connotations of the 'concept',
i.e. intentionality, planning, accountability, etc. Even within
the human context there is no necessity to have always regress
to the agent as an active person. In a trivial case like pointing
with a finger, the finger is an agent and the pointing is an
act, though in the accomplished act the finger *qua* agent and
the pointing *qua* act, coalesce. If we may comment on the deri-
vation of the German *Handlung* from hand, we see that human

acts were conceived in the first place as related to an organ of the body, and thus the organ is a limited agent, viewed from the point of view of the occurrence of, and even observed as involved in the act. Hence the introduction of the concept of agent, the procedure to which we referred before as 'metaphysical deduction', is guided by an attempt to go beyond a limited or diffuse agent to a comprehensive agent — though the latter step involves problems of will, intentionality, etc.

Yet the realm of acts and deeds within the human scope does not always allow for the identification of the agent, even when we assume that agents are involved in the acts. An obvious example is the behaviour of a mass of individuals, when the character of the act — like demonstrations, violent outbursts — does not allow for the identification of single agents. We discern occurrences *qua* acts since the occurences are e.g. outbursts of violence and not tropical rains, but it may be difficult or even impossible to discern the continuous line from the agents to the act. It is, on the one hand, evident that human beings are involved in the acts but, on the other hand, the regression from the acts to the causative position of the actors or agents is more than difficult. We discern a particular sort of activity — not one which enables a clear distinction between cause and effect but a situation where the causative factors are to some extent at least identical with their acts. Several additional conclusions follow from this observation.

As we have seen, the presupposition for the very demarcation of the field of acts lies in the distinction between the given and the changed reality where the change occurred through intervention. Even when we cannot identify agents the intervention is there. Thus the distinction between reality and intervention in it is broader than the distinction between the agent confronting reality and the changes he introduces in it. Hence, the duality between reality and change by intervention is our phenomenological point of departure. There emerges here the question of the agent *vis-à-vis* intervention, once intervention has been undertaken. Again the introduction of the concept of agent follows the line of regression in which the human agent, in the integrative sense of the term, is to some extent the last link in the chain of regression, though it is always possible to ask the question: who is the agent behind the agent — parallel to the question: who is the custodian of the custodians? These questions indicate the line toward an infinite regression, while the introduction of the concept of agent is an attempt to pursue the regression up to a certain point and then present, sometimes at least, perhaps through introspection, a link which will arrest the infinite regression.

The impact of introspection or self-reflection is significant, not only from the point of view of delineating the sphere of the human agent, but also from the point of view of the acts and deeds as such. Since acts and deeds are changes introduced into reality, we may ask the question: how is it that precisely these acts and deeds have been introduced into reality? When we follow the line, or the course, of reality as such, we refer to the inner rhythm of reality and its structure, based on laws. But once additions which do not follow the line of reality are brought in, we can question the inner logic of the changes introduced. The concept of the agent in the human sense is one of the explanations why precisely these deeds and acts did occur and others did not. We read here from introspection the first observation, namely, that the human agent perceives reality as open, that is to say, as capable of absorbing a deed, and that he perceives himself, to some extent, as open too, namely, as being capable of producing acts and deeds in more than one direction. He can walk and sit, he can operate and produce certain tools. Some of the directions may coincide, as, for instance, making certain moves and handling a tool, but some of the acts may exclude each other, as, for instance, sitting excludes running, or using one's hands for making a tool excludes using one's hands for painting. Hence from the point of view of the agent and his performance, the openness of reality is counterbalanced by the contraction of the line or channel of deeds and acts performed. Here again, the question referring to the position of the agent leads to the supplementary question of the motivations for the contraction, and the aspect of choice emerges in the context. A choice is of course related to the motivation of the agent, when we regress from his performance to his 'inner' life. In any case, the inverse relationship between openness and contraction leads us to the assumption that within the human sphere there is, and can be, a multiplicity of lines of action or of different deeds. One of the usual descriptions is relevant in the present context, namely, that within the animal world the line of acts is predetermined or prescribed whilst the human world is characterized by its openness to various lines of action, both impromptu individual acts at certain moments and acts methodically planned, where one act is meant to support a subsequent act. Here, too, as suggested before, we have to distinguish between the openness of the field and the choice *qua* decision; even when we grant the impact of decision in the direction of taking one line of action out of other possible lines, what determines the choice is still an open question, i.e. whether the choice is a mere decision or whether it is prompted by outside factors. This is only to say that an attempt toward a demarcation of the area of acts does not necessarily coincide with the controversy between determinism and indeterminism.

(3)

Inasmuch as the question of choice arises in this context, the question of knowledge arises as well. It may sound, as a paradox, but the cognitive ingredient is phenomenologically to some extent the primary ingredient compared with the ingredient of choice. We assume that choice is a way of explaining the contraction present in the deed performed – e.g. writing and not handling. But the discernment of reality, reality being the encompassing locus for the deed, let alone the discernment of the openness enabling the deed or making it an occurrence responding to the openness – all these presuppose an awareness or a knowledge, an orientation in reality, including an orientation to which a certain deed is supposedly a proper response. There is a time to walk and a time to handle, and these are not always just performances; they are related to the situation at stake. In a certain situation we speak, and in another situation we write a letter. These are deeds performed according to what is suitable to, or possible in, a situation. Moreover, the dependence on knowledge – and technological civilization to be dealt with is a most telling example — opens up new areas for acts and deeds, at least in the sense that the areas discerned become objects for deeds or interventions. In this sense, the cognitive attitude is a presupposition or a condition for the acts and deeds. Here again, the aspect of agent enters the context. But the knowledge presupposed for the background of the agent's deed is not simply identical with the personal knowledge *qua* orientation of the individual agent. There is accumulated knowledge which finds expression, for instance, in day-to-day behaviour. Even when the behaving person does not know the code of our behaviour or its reasons and its history, the pattern itself guides him in it.

Many aspects of inter-personal conduct and etiquette carry in themselves acts and deeds following patterns accompanied and guided by knowledge of the external aspects of the pattern without necessarily assuming knowledge in the anthropological or historical sense of the term. *Mutatis mutandis* the same structure applies to acts and deeds outside the patterns of a tradition in the area of, for instance, computers. Persons handling computers do not necessarily know game theory or the basic aspects of computers in their relations to mathematics or to logic. The non-personal knowledge is presupposed and in a sense is embodied in the computer. The person handling the computer knows only a segment of the whole structure; he is not unlike the person knowing the pattern of behaviour without knowing the meaning of the pattern or its dimension. Hence there exists a scale of knowledge surrounding acts, starting probably from what we call vague orientation, going up to knowledge of codes, as segments, and concluding in the ever broadening horizon of knowledge which, on the one hand accompanies acts and on the other may give rise to additional acts and deeds to occur or to be performed. The positing which is the outcome of acts and deeds, namely, the positing of facts in this sense, presupposes knowledge of the reality in which facts are posited and it presupposes the knowledge which finds expression, at least sometimes, in the deed performed. Here, too, we realize that acts and deeds occupy an in-between position between reality and knowledge.

Up to this point, we have been concerned with the dimension

of acts *vis-à-vis* reality, having subsumed acts and deeds under the broad notion of intervention. But there is an additional aspect to acts and deeds, namely, the inter-human aspect, which we will now consider.

(4)

The other human being, in the singular or plural, appears to the acting human being, in the first place, as part of reality. Inasmuch as acts intervene in reality, they encounter or are faced with the presence of other acts from which we, in similar way, as referring to ourselves, assume the position of the agents. First, we perhaps encounter outcomes or products of acts, traces of the presence of human beings, and in different ways, similar to those applied to the assertion of the *alter ego*, we assume that the products or traces are outcomes of acts not performed by ourselves, *ergo* they are performed by other human beings. Having said this, we may add that, as a matter of fact and as part of reality, we encounter not only outcomes of acts nor do we only watch acts being performed. We encounter human beings and, at the same time, their responses to our very presence in reality, as well as to the acts which we perform, their outcomes, achievements and failures. From the point of view of acts as interventions in reality, the first encounter with a human being or with a plurality of human beings is perceived as an obstacle. The human being is there and thus, in a way, hampers the *élan* of our action or contracts the space of our activity. But, unlike opaque pieces of reality, the present human being is a 'responding obstacle', he expresses his view or reaction when we overstep our boundaries and encroach on him. He may withdraw from the space of our activity, but he may be resilient and respond by pushing us back and thus contracting the initial space of our action. The response, unlike the inertia of matter, creates *pari passu* an inter-human context. Hence acts and deeds, while facing reality and together with this other human beings, intervene in reality, on the one hand, and absorb responses in the inter-human sphere, on the other. In a way, the primary response is a negative response — and in referring to primacy we do not refer to the chronological connotation of primacy but to its thematic connotation, i.e. to the minimum of interaction implied. That minimum is the response emanating from the very presence of, namely, the response embodied in, the obstacle. As we have seen, the obstacle can be the presence as such and can be its active manifestation as reacting to our intervention. But when the presence of the other human beings is assessed from the point of view of action, two modes of re-action become available or, put differently, the interpretation by the actor of the response as a partial manifestation of the presence of other human beings may take shape in two major directions. We may call them participation and division. Parti-cipation implies mainly the shaping of the inter-human context in the direction of a common effort, such as helping to push a car which has stalled. Division is a different mode of the inter-personal context since it amounts to division of work or division of roles for the sake of a common achievement, like, for in-stance, — to take a very primitive example — the division of work within the household and the extramural work. Both modes of a joint enterprise presuppose certain constant factors in the inter-human context. The most basic presupposition is that the intentionality towards intervening in reality is a common human feature and can be directed into the major channels of the inter-human encounter. It can be put differently: the response al-ready experienced on the elementary level of the inter-human encounter now becomes a response in the direction of a common effort or division of labour for the sake of a common achievement — as is the case in our example, namely, that subsistence is achieved through a division between that which goes on within the walls of the household and that which is earned outside those walls.

To be sure, different directions of acts still occur within the framework of reality and concurrently are meant to change reali-ty. But this time, not by scattered deeds or by the continuous deed of a single individual but by deeds interwoven with the inter-human context. Still, the access to reality or to the factual situation looms large in any inter-human context. One of the expressions of the centrality of the factual reality, from the point of view of acts and deeds, is their evaluation according to the yardstick usually called 'practical'. The application of that yardstick amounts to an evaluation of the deeds from the point of view of their being capable of integration into reality, or, put differently, whether or not they adequately take into account the resistance of reality or, by the same token, the openness of reality. That which is non-practical amounts to ignoring elements of reality or falsely interpreting the basic presupposition of the openness of reality. Thus, the practical consideration is an evaluation of the act from the vantage point of its relation to reality. Therefore we could say that practicality is the minimal evaluation of an act. We are not evaluating it from the perspective of whether or not the objective has been achieved, let alone whether or not it should be achieved. We are evaluating the primary component of the act, namely, its suitability from the point of view of the factual data — and these may be both data of reality in the broad sense and data of the presence of other human beings. It is impractical to use water as a tool as it is impractical to assemble infants to push a car. Because practicality and impracticality are related to the interpretation of reality and to the adequate integration of that interpretation into the acts or deeds we perform, a broader meaning of practicality and impracticality is rendered when we speak about utopias, plans which are of a fictional character, etc. In this sense practicality implies not the proper consideration of the plain facts of reality but the very push towards reality. Hence those who are impractical are 'dreamers' lacking the necessary concern for the dimension of reality. We encounter here a blurring of several distinctions: The very striving towards reality is viewed as an activity, though obviously building utopias is an activity too. Activity, in its limited sense, refers to the gap between planning and reality while passivity is listed as characterizing only intentions, outlines, alternatives, etc. Hence, in one sense the very intentionality toward reality is already an activity, whereas in another sense, only performance is an activity. The distinction between the intentional and the performing aspect of acts has deep roots in the history of philosophical interpretations of actions in general and moral actions in particular, since, as we shall see later, the aspect of intentionality or intentions may be fundamental for the modes of action called moral and not quite as fundamental for other modes of action like labour, etc. Typologically speaking, the importance of moral acts and deeds for the broad understanding of the domain of acts lies precisely in the question of whether or not there is a continuous transition from intentions to deeds, or what is the impact of the intentions on the deeds and, therefore, whether or not there exist adequate intentions serving as necessary and sufficient conditions for the acts performed. Obviously, the Socratic tradition represents an interpretation of acts and deeds — to be sure, moral ones — where a line of continuity exists from knowing what has to be done, intending to do it, and the actual deed performed. We take here the Socratic interpretation of moral deeds only as a model for the purpose of presenting, at least, the possibility of viewing deeds in different contexts, that is to say, we ask the question whether the absence of that continuity or total *Gestalt* would point to a different type or types of acts and deeds as one of their phenomenological features.

There is an additional reason for our introduction of the Socratic model into the preliminary characterization of the domain of deeds. Once the model guiding us is the Socratic *Gestalt*, the assertion of the agent seems to be plausible. If acts and deeds can be viewed *prima facie* as scattered and fragmentary, the intention guiding the deed is, at least, not visible as is the act. Intention can be turned into the guiding or prompting factor of the deed, and thus in a way the deed can be viewed as a means to the end prescribed by the intention. This applies *a fortiori* to the additional component, namely knowledge. Since knowledge guides the intention, it cannot be impersonal knowledge which exists, somewhere, as a treasure of information accessible to those who want or would like to know. The knowledge referred to or presupposed in the Socratic *Gestalt* is the knowledge of a knower who gives meaning to the intention, turning the intention into both the guiding content and the factor pushing in the direction of performance of the actual deed. It is from this consideration that, even when we do not assume the primacy of the moral deeds within the broad sphere of acts and deeds, the interconnection between acts and agents becomes primarily manifest in that sphere. In other words, inasmuch as we started with the inter-human aspect on the level of responses, the plane of moral acts leads us not into the general direction of responses but into the direction of initiating by and through knowledge and intention.

There is an additional aspect to this juxtaposition of responses and intentions. We have seen the aspect of evaluation as implied in every act from the point of view of the responsive attitude and the point of view of practicality *qua* admissibility into reality. But the aspect of evaluation is accompanied by an aspect of knowledge and we can say — the more we evaluate the more we know and the more we know the more we evaluate. Within the inter-human context there is indeed present the aspect of practicality which we pointed out before: who, for instance, can participate in a common effort and on whom can we rely in the division of labour? But once we want to do something for our fellow-man, for instance help him in his predicament, e.g. cure his poor health, the aspect of practicality is there but is not sufficient as a yardstick for the evaluation of our performance or its objective. For the purpose of help or curing we have to know many facts related to the fellow-man: his past history, his life-style, his performances, etc. The accumulation of knowledge calls for a concomitant evaluation. For instance, when we try to cure somebody without having sufficient knowledge, we may do him harm. Thus we are exposed to an evaluation which, though it contains the aspect of practicality, goes beyond it, when, for instance, our objective has not been achieved or, even on the contrary, the situation has been made worse. But we evaluate both the components of knowledge implied and the intention, namely, whether or not the agent attempting to cure is prompted by concern for his patient. Sometimes, in the line of evaluation, we may even follow a distinction between the lack of achievement calling for a negative evaluation and the investment of the proper intention calling for a positive evaluation. The more components there are in an action, the more diversified will its evaluation be. We are sometimes led to an additional step related to the difference between an individual act and the broader norm which might find its manifestation in that act. For instance, the concern for human beings is a broader norm than the concern for Paul or John. When we find a person willing to cure only Paul or John, we may evaluate him negatively because his focused concern ought to be grounded in a universal or broad norm. Thus, even exceptions are evaluated by the reference to a broader norm.

Our discussion of the Socratic interpretation of the relationship pertaining between knowledge and act is meant to serve two considerations: In the first place, the Socratic position can be viewed as a radical model for the *Gestalt* characteristic of the inner connections leading from knowledge to acts. Hence other modes of acts, where knowledge is not so prominent, will be conceived as softer versions of the Socratic model or, put differently, the Socratic model is an ideal type of the fundamental relationship prevailing between the component of knowledge and the component of deed. According to that ideal type, knowledge *per se*, where the knower is fully identified with that which he knows, leads directly to a deed or to an act. The softer versions of the structure of knowledge and deed will be characterized by a lack of this straight continuity from knowledge to deed. We may plan to do something and do it. But we can also, as we say, play with ideas and not implement them. In these cases there exists, at least, the possibility that the plan is not carried through because a different or countervailing knowledge becomes prominent, as is the case when we plan something and do not enact it since we realize that it would not be 'practical' to engage in the enactment.

(5)

There is an additional consideration prompting us to apply the Socratic model in an attempt to outline a theory of acts and deeds. That consideration can be described as the aspect of evaluation or justification present in the analysis of acts and deeds. Here again the Socratic position can be viewed as a radical model for the inter-texture of evaluation and acts since Socrates referred to the knowledge of what is good as becoming a virtue, eventually manifesting itself in the actual deed. The configuration of knowledge and deeds refers here to a singular aspect of knowledge which is the good or goodness. Hence, softer versions of acts and deeds in their grounding in, or relationship to, knowledge are those where knowledge is broadly conceived as awareness of situations, facts, laws of nature, etc. The deeds enacted are related to that scope of knowledge but cannot be viewed as being a direct continuation of it, since knowledge is taken in a more neutral sense – as enabling action and guiding it, but not directly motivating it. But once knowledge is not normative in the first place, where or from which direction does the aspect of evaluation of the deed or its eventual justification emerge? This question has to be discussed from several aspects.

The first possibility is to apply the awareness of a principle pertaining to the acts of knowledge by translating them into interventions in the surrounding reality. The difference is clear, and we have referred to it at various points in our preceding analysis. To know an object does not mean to change it. On the contrary, to know an object is to state the qualities or the relation of the object as it is. A change affecting the object changes the subject matter of knowledge. That difference between the 'act of knowing', as the term has it, and the acts of changing, cannot be obliterated. Hence the application of the component of act which we realized in the area of knowledge cannot be naively accepted in the area of deeds. Yet, in the description presented, there is a lesson which we learn from the area of knowledge. Simply to state a state of affairs adequately calls for refraining from changing it. Thus there is a built-in norm guiding our cognitive approach: to remain adequate presupposes refraining from change. Hence we amplify our lesson by assuming that wherever change is introduced, it has to be justified, deliberately or not, at least by way of a comparison with the cognitive situation. Precisely since a change alters the state of affairs, we can address ourselves to the change or, as is usually done, to the agent intervening in reality and bringing about a change, asking him why or for what reason he introduced this change. There is a sort of primacy implied in the cognitive attitude, precisely because that attitude leaves reality as it is; hence non-intervention in reality is systematically a primary attitude as compared with the practical attitude. From this point of view there is no essential difference between what the tradition called *praxis* and what is called *poiesis*, namely, between acts and deeds referring to one's will or character and acts and deeds referring to actual intervention in nature, e.g. by building houses and bridges. Both directions of action change reality and presuppose a knowledge of it, even when we assume, following the Socratic line, that the knowledge of the norm of goodness is essential for shaping the reality of will and character. Both directions are indeed interventions, even when we grant the difference: *praxis* is an intervention which does not become visible in self-contained products of action while *poiesis* is consummated in products of sorts — and here again the house or the bridge built are suitable examples.

Once we go beyond the mere discernment of the facts, either of the psyche or of the data of nature, and change them, either by giving them shape or by producing artifacts, we face the question: why did we perform the action? In this case, for instance, the norm of goodness becomes the justification for our deed in influencing the character or the soul. The achievement is the very shaping of the character. The component of achievement is not altogether missing, as we are sometimes inclined to say rashly when emphasizing the aspect of intention. What is characteristic of that sort of action is the coalescence of the norm with the achievement. The achievement, in turn, becomes evaluated or justified because of the norm, and the norm is viewed, at least partly, from the point of view of its impact leading towards achievement. *Mutatis mutandis* the same reasoning applies to products and to actions leading to them. We ask what purpose does a product serve, for instance, whether it is meant to be beautiful as an artifact or functional as serving a useful purpose, such as living in a house, crossing a river, etc. The question can be raised by the agent and can thus accompany his intention, or it can be raised by the responding fellow-man who encounters the change introduced. Comparing the awareness of the given reality with the change meant to be introduced, or actually introduced, leads to the question which we render *cui bono*? — where obviously the term *bonum* connotes both the norm of goodness and the objective meant to be achieved. Were it not for the primacy of cognition or of the cognitive attitude, the question of justifying the change or intervention would not arise or, in other words, since we presuppose the given reality, we are asked to justify our intervention in it.

Yet there is a peculiar dialectical relationship pertaining between the cognitive attitude exemplifying the non-intervening one and the practical and poietical attitude exemplifying the intervening one. Inasmuch as we compare the cognitive attitude with the attitude of doing and assume that non-intervention is essential for the cognitive attitude, we justify, to some extent, the cognitive attitude from the perspective of the practical one. We are led to analyze the *raison d'être* of the sphere of knowledge realizing that once adequacy or truth are the principles of knowledge they prescribe the curb on changing the state of affairs which is the subject matter of our knowledge. Thus, to some extent, we apply the structure of acts and deeds to the structure of knowledge, emphasizing the difference between the two spheres. We may suggest the following reasoning at this juncture: systematically we presuppose the primacy of reality and, therefore, also the primacy of the cognitive attitude, as intentionality *par excellence* towards reality. But experientially or empirically, we start with acts and deeds amplified systematically or terminologically, as interventions or changes in reality. Thus we impose the experiential primacy on what is systematically primary. In this sense we would say that not to do is just the same as to do. As we commonly say — not to decide is a decision, too.

The aspect of evaluation or justification has also to be considered from another point of view: that of the agent and not necessarily that of the resulting achievement or product. The reference to the agent emerges in the following context: since knowing has its built-in principle, namely, that of adequacy with the state of affairs or, more generally, that of truth, in certain situations we may ask the question: how is it that the principle has not been realized, namely, that the state of affairs has not become known, deciphered and adequately stated? We can list different explanations for the failure in accomplishing the adequate statement from the point of view of a subject matter which is a new phenomenon for whose identification we lack the necessary co-ordinates. But sometimes at least we may explain the failure by a lack of precision on the part of the knower who has identified a phenomenon without possessing adequate grounding or, last but not least, by his lack of intention to state the subject matter adequately. In those cases the failure amounts not only to a fallacy but also to a falseness, lack of truthfulness or even a lie. Thus the cognitive situation, once its correlative structure is discerned, i.e. that between knowing which is carried by a knower and the subject matter which is about to be known, leads us by way of looking for an explanation to an evaluation which, in some cases, amounts to a justification of what has occurred, and in other cases to a censure or condemnation of it.

Essentially, the same structure applies to the realm of acts and deeds. We can evaluate the achievement or the result and sometimes even disregard the intentionality or intention. But sometimes we are led to evaluate the intention or the norm, and this happens again mainly in situations of mishaps or failures, as is the case in the cognitive sphere. If a bridge or a house fall down, that occurrence is the point of departure not only of the evaluation of the product whose failure is visible but also leads to an evaluation of the process which led to the mishap, for instance whether the planning was adequate, whether the cognitive description of the data of nature was adequate, but also whether the planners and builders were honest, that is to say, concerned with the adequacy of the product and its function or purpose, or were perhaps negligent, etc. etc. Both in the cognitive and in the practical field evaluation is triggered off by the situation; we perform an analysis step by step — which is a continuous regression from the lack of the aspired achievement to the agent. Yet, even when we begin in our experience from a negative achievement, and because of this we perform the regressive analysis landing in the area of the agent, the same applies to positive achievements, that is to say, to true statements as adequate ones, or to working achievements once we refer to products. Obviously, since we land eventually on the level of the agent, we face new difficulties due to the complexity of the concept of the agent, and the various elements from which he is essentially composed. Here our explanation follows the usual line, namely, we point to an explaining factor in spite of the fact that this factor in turn may call for a new line of explanation. This logic applies to the explanation of natural occurrences as it does to the explanation of historical ones.

(6)

Our description and explication of the realm of acts and deeds poses, as a matter of fact, a basic question, namely, whether we are at all permitted to refer here to a realm, or whether we are referring to scattered acts and deeds whose characteristic feature is not their place in a realm but their intervention in reality which comprises both itself and the intervening acts. Moreover, the very presupposition of reality in our approach to an outline of the nature of acts has as its corollary the intervening and not the independent character of acts, facing reality and establishing itself in an independent or semi-independent sphere.

This basic description of acts calls for an antithetic analysis of the most prominent systematic philosophical attempt to outline the sphere of acts as a self-contained sphere with an intrinsic structure of its own. We refer here to Hegel's theory of spirit (*Geist*) and to its dialectical consequence, Marx's theory of *praxis*. Naturally it has to be observed that Hegel did not only assume the self-contained character of spirit, grounding acts in it. He also assumed the comprehensive character of spirit, that is to say, that reality itself is spirit. But for the sake of our analysis, in the limited sense of the term, it is enough to deal with the comprehensive character of the sphere of deeds, subsumed under the heading of 'objective spirit' (*der objektive Geist*).

It is in this context that we have to ask ourselves the preliminary question regarding the very systematic possibility of placing acts and deeds in the orbit of spirit and involving them in the essence of spirit. It seems to be warranted to assume that the *tertium comparationis* between spirit in general and deeds lies, according to Hegel, in the very essence of spirit, not in something which is at rest but rather in something that is absolutely restless or which is pure activity (*die reine Tätig-keit*).[1] Obviously, the reference to the essence of restlessness is a more metaphoric expression than the subsequent one, namely, pure activity. Here we could suggest an attempt towards integration of the Heraclitian element and *praxis* which ceases to be one of the manifestations of the spirit and becomes its very essence. But precisely through that attempt, *praxis* itself ceases to be a limited attitude and manifestation and becomes the very essence of the agent and its prompting character — of spirit. Absolute self-determination[2] becomes essentially identical with activity; the manifestation of self-determination and activity amounts to development which in turn has the character of expression as well as a teleological character, namely, intending to reach an objective and reaching it eventually — which in turn amounts to the identity between spirit and reality. In any case, the absorption by spirit of activity makes acts and deeds, as interventions in reality, already grounded in the comprehensive nature of the spirit. The particular manifestation of spirit in the area of acts and deeds, in the limited sense, amounts to moral philosophy or to analysis of moral acts, to the analysis of work and labour as related to social deeds, to the analysis of politics, and eventually philosophy of history as an analysis of the historical process and manifestations emerging from it. Grounding deeds in their limited sense in spirit as the totality of self-determination and development, immediately presents a yardstick for grading these deeds: morality *qua Sittlichkeit* is conceived as the perfection of the objective spirit, that is to say, as the truth of the subjective and objective spirit itself.[3] Deeds and acts are no longer grounded in the individual agent but are externalizations (*Entäusserungen*) or objectivizations of spirit as a substance.

---

1. *Enzyklopädie der Philosophischen Wissenschaften*, & 378, *Zusatz*. On Hegel's concept of spirit see the present author's: *On Spirit, An Interpretation of Hegel, Hegel-Studien*, herausgegeben von Friedrich Nicolin und Otto Pöggeler, 1980, pp. 199ff.
2. *Ibid.*, § 442, *Zusatz*.
3. *Ibid.*, § 513.

One basic aspect of Hegel's view is the spheric or overriding character of deeds. As such, they are in the first place involved in a logic of development. They are indeed manifestations. The individual deeds are initially integrated into sub-spheres: work, the political sphere, the moral sphere. The structure of each of those spheres determines and impregnates the particular and singular deeds. Once Hegel introduced *praxis* into spirit, he opened the way for turning it around, namely, introducing spirit into praxis. This is what Marx attempted to achieve, since for Marx man is a being involved in the process of discourse (*Auseinandersetzung*) with nature, which in turn has the character of expression or objectivization (*Vergegenständlichung*), or production of an objectivized world (*Erzeugung einer gegenständlichen Welt*). But that production, which amounts to the full activity of life, is the process of labour or work and not the process of spirit in the sense explicated before in Hegel's sense.[4] There is a symmetry between the Hegelian notion of spirit and Marx's notion of labour, since both attempt to present an overriding agent expressing himself in the process and imbued by definition with the element of activity. Both views are parallel, since they conceive of activity as finding its consummation in the very manifestation of its latent content, though Hegel conceives of that manifestation as being essentially aimed at the enhancement of the inner content of spirit, while for Marx the manifestation is consummated in the creation of the objective world. But the parallelism goes even further, since for both Hegel and Marx activity amounts to creativity, i.e. to the creation of the world; both do not presuppose reality but trace the emergence of reality out of the activity. The difference between the two conceptions, as we noted earlier, lies in the first place in Marx's replacement of Hegel's spirit by labour, or in other words, in making labour the activity instead of identifying spirit with activity. Along with this difference comes a second one, namely, that for Hegel *Entäusserung* as objectivization is only an interim step in the process of activity which

4. *Ökonomisch-philosophische Manuskripte*, Marx-Engels's *Werke*, Ergänzungsband I, Berlin, 1968, p. 574; as well as *Das Kapital Werke*, Bd. 2, 3, 9. 179.

eventually culminates in the return of the objective and its integration in the absolute. While for Marx the interplay between work and objectivization becomes an ultimate stage in development since the metabolic exchange between man and nature, to use his term (*Stoffwechsel*), is the ultimate feature of human reality.

Granting all these differences and their nuances we have to realize that in terms of individual acts Marx maintained the Hegelian structure, namely, that acts are essentially integrated in an overriding process and are thus imbued with a logic of the process. *Praxis* is a historical sum-total of acts; it creates a momentum, there is an *Unterbau* and an *Überbau*, and in any case, there is no embracing reality which we face and try to restructure in a fragmentary way. On the contrary, there is a process imposing itself on reality, either turning reality into spirit in Hegel's sense or creating a human enclave within which we, through deeds grounded in praxis, find our access to nature. It is perhaps significant that Marx does not refer to reality but to nature, thus even terminologically indicating a limited sphere within reality and not reality in its broadest contours.[5]

It is at this point that the present analysis takes exception from the two great systematic attempts to impose an overriding structure on acts and deeds, be it a spiritual one or one of *praxis*. Our contention is that from the point of view of the agent there is only an intervention in the surroundings, or even only an attempt to intervene in it. Even the introduction of the notion of the agent has a regressive character. We start out from acts and deeds, and one attempt at integrating them is to relate them to the intervening actor or agent. The arguments in favour of that integration are in turn related to an introversion to the context of responses between human beings. But even when that integration is achieved, it is from the point of view of acts and not of the products of the acts. The products become estranged from the agent; the effects of his acts and deeds are beyond his control, even when he takes upon himself

---

5. Consult in Manfred Riedel's *Studien zu Hegel's Rechtsphilosophie*, Suhrkamp Verlag, 1969, 'Objektiver Geist und praktische Philosophie', pp. 11ff.

the accountability for the deeds and their products. Precisely since the products get involved in reality and thus become integrated into the context of reality, the accountability relates to intentions or to deliberate effects, but not to the trans-intentional fate of deeds and acts, i.e. their effects. Once there is no continuity between the agent, the deed and the product, and each of the ingredients dwells as it were in its own semi-secluded sphere, it is impossible to erase the differences between the ingredients and their spheres and to conceive of them as being inherent in an overriding realm of spirit or praxis. It is fairly easy to assume that all acts and deeds performed here and now are manifestations of a total substance *qua* spirit, or of a total activity *qua* praxis. But it remains unexplained how spirit manifests itself precisely in the acts and deeds performed here and now, or how praxis becomes singularized, or let us say individualized, in the particular acts performed by particular individuals. Again it is rather easy to say that individuals are executives of a world spirit (*Geschäftsführer des Geistes*), but precisely that position calls for prudent analysis in reaching awareness of a situation here and now. Should all these components — which to some extent can be subsummed under the heading of practicality — be integrated in spirit or praxis and exist on the same level as the scaling of modes of activity or the direction of world history? There remains the question of the traces left in reality by acts and deeds, the absorbing character of reality in the sense that even intervening acts and their outcomes *qua* products do not remain on the level of activities but become part and parcel of reality. This aspect cannot be explained by the totalistic mode of explaining and placing acts and deeds. Any integration of them in structures is essentially a *post-factum* analysis and explanation, though the *post-factum* approach is eventually turned into its reverse by making the *a priori* structure the guiding principle of acts and not the reverse. Once we maintain the correlation between acts and reality, we cannot be oblivious of the particular character of acts by making them parallel to reality or elevating them to the level of creators of reality. This is why we shall follow a different, far less presumptious line, suggesting a distinction between acts intervening in reality and those creating

a sphere aside of reality. Labour and play will be two para-
digmatic modes of activity, and they will lead us to the question
as of the placing of moral acts.[6]

6. See Robert Ware: 'Acts and Action', *The Journal of Philosophy*, Vol. LXV, 13,
July 19, 1973, pp. 403ff.
From the phenomenological literature we mention:
a. Gerart Husserl: *Person, Sache, Verhalten.* Zwei phänomenologische Studien,
Klostermann, Frankfurt a. M., 1969.
b. F.J.J. Buytendijk: *Allgemeine Theorie der menschlichen Haltung*, Springer-
Verlag, Berlin/Göttingen/Heidelberg, 1956.
c. *Phänomenologie und Praxis*, ed. Ernst W. Orth, Phänomenologische Forschungen,
Bd. 3, Karl Alber, Freiburg/München, 1976.

CHAPTER THREE

WORK AND LABOUR

(1)

In attempting to analyse the nature of work we are bound to be aware of the paradox inherent in such an attempt. Each of us knows the actual meaning of work. But in describing the activity embodied in work we face difficulties, not only since such a description must aim at an integration of perspectives, but also because we have to adequately express our own deep-rooted and even pervasive experience. This is a case where articulation is in reverse proportion to our day-to-day realization or awareness.

Terminologically it has to be observed that in many languages different words exist, epitomizing traditional distinctions, for that sort of activity which we are now attempting to analyse, chiefly distinguishing between *laborare* and *facere*. In English these appear as 'labour' and 'work', and in French as *travail* and *œuvre*. We are aware of the fact that references to 'work' and 'labour' very often call for a concomitant evaluation, mainly when work or labour are related to trouble and extertion: to toil means to work and to labour. This evaluation of labour seems to be so predominant that we find, for instance, in Kant the statement that labour is a business or activity which is disagreeable on its own account because it is drudgery. It is only attractive because of its results, e.g. as pay (*Lohn*).[1] In the present analysis we shall use 'work' for the activity, and labour to indicate the effort and toil inherent in it.

---

1. *Kritik d. Urteilskraft*, ed. Vorländer, Meiner Verlag, Leipzig, 1924, para. 43, p. 156; James W. Meredith's transl. at Clarendon Press, Oxford, p. 164.

It is not the intention of the following analysis to dwell on the distinctions between work and labour, let alone to impose on the description any evaluation which, justified as it may be, can still only accompany the description and not replace it or appear jointly with it. We shall try to anchor work and labour as an activity in the position of man in his environment or in the world, and even perhaps, in stronger terms, to see work as related to the sustenance of the organism in the environment transported to the level of human existence. Our elementary point of departure is that an organism is not self-sufficient and, therefore, is bound for its subsistence to find its *locus* in the environment and to bring the environment, or at least some of its ingredients, into its own sphere or to adapt itself to the environment. Both adaptation of and incorporation in the organism are activities — whether of an instinctual character or of a character related to and grounded in planning and deliberation. What applies to organisms in general applies to the human organism in particular. But, given the nature of human existence, this organism is involved in certain deliberations or is subject to interventions. Deeds and acts are thus prompted by organic life. Inasmuch as they can be isolated for the sake of analysis they may take the form of a singular mode of intervention which we describe as work and labour. These are grounded in the need of the organism to survive through intervention in the environment, and can, thus, be viewed as supplementing the lack of self-sufficiency which is our point of departure in the present analysis. Work is a tool for the sake of counterbalancing the lack of self-sufficiency and is, thus, instrumental or a means; but work is at the same time the prolongation of the life of the organism or of the basic human existence, enabling it to maintain itself in a given environment. Such work is simultaneously grounded in a need or a necessity, and is accompanied by an expectation that the need will be fulfilled or that it will be satisfied according to expectation. The expectation of the fulfilment which, as such, prompts the activity but already looks forward to its outcome, explains the fact that in many linguistic expressions 'work' connotes both the activity and the result. Moreover, since the result is anticipated, the achievement of the result becomes a fulfilment. Thus it is accompanied by pleasure or satisfaction which, in turn, are attitudes or states of mind occurring whenever the expectation and the achievement coincide.

(2)

Since we can take work in a broad sense as an activity accomplishing something, or as an endeavour in two senses, i.e. the activity and the *opus*, in order to delineate the sphere of labour and work it is desirable to place it in close proximity to the organism. This is a deliberate contraction of the meaning of work and labour, once we accept, for instance, that play is also labour, or that, e.g. participation in elections has at least a component of effort and thus is labour as well. The contraction needs a justification; that justification lies in the organism and its needs; that is to say, in most cases to work is to work for one's livelihood. Hence we single out, in the first place, the goal of work — work is not an activity as such, though it can be understood in this way. It has a teleological character: sustenance, subsistence, maintenance of the organism and its life, and at the same time it is motivated by certain discernable needs, for instance, the need for food or shelter, while the satisfaction of those needs cannot be achieved and safeguarded unless there is a directedness towards that satisfaction, or until the work is done. This character of work immediately presents, on the level of the elementary essence of work as it is understood in this context, a particular synthesis characteristic of work — the synthesis between the broad goal which is sustenance or livelihood, and the specific aim related to the meeting or satisfaction of specific needs. Livelihood cannot be safeguarded unless specific needs are met. Hence work has an end in livelihood as well as secondary ends in the satisfaction of specific needs. The synthetic character of work becomes prominent in two additional features which imply a presupposed agent or worker. The first is related to the fact that work is, in the first place, a directed intervention in the environment. It is sowing, or reaping, or modelling a tool. But at the same time there is at least a tacit anticipation that the externalized activity will be brought back into the sphere of the worker, and will fulfil a function which he expects — either directly by satisfying his hunger, or indirectly by providing him with a tool to achieve an end that calls for a tool as a means. There is no externalization in work unless there is the ultimate internalization. Here again we see the *locus* for the feelings of pleasure and satisfaction which relate to the introversion following the externalization.

Hence — and this leads us to our second observation — even on the elementary level of work, the agent is not confined to the role of an actor accomplishing the particular deed for the sake of the role in which he is active. He is an actor endowed with what we may call the capacity for resonance, for echoing the deed and translating the echo into the sphere of his existence, including the feeling or awareness of satisfaction. Though we have deliberately limited the definition of sphere of work to intervention for the sake of sustenance, we realize that the distinction between the activity of the body and the 'mental resonance' cannot be as clearly delineated as we sometimes tend to make it.

(3)

At this point an additional aspect of work must be emphasized. In the most elementary sense, an act of intervention is composed of many acts, as for instance, sowing is composed of many sub-actions. But in our characterization of an act or its direction we deliberately disregard the components and refer to an integrated act. We do so since the sub-acts would probably not present to us the meaning of the act, its direction, goal, etc. Only the *Gestalt* presents the meaning or is functional from the aspect of the act to be achieved. But once the functional consideration becomes important, work is not only a sum-total of sub-acts but can be a chain of acts, as is the case with the making of tools. Tools are made in order to achieve a goal and they are functionally motivated in a very strict sense. But to make a tool is already to accomplish a work. Concentration on the end goal cannot release us from the deliberate attempt to create a tool for the sake of attaining this ultimate goal; the tool itself already becomes a goal. It is no accident that concentration on making tools can preoccupy us to the extent that it may sometimes lead to what we call estrangement, that is to say, that somehow we become oblivious of the ultimate goal and concentrate on the tool as a goal. It goes without saying that the refinement of tools calls for more and more concentration, and work, to put it this way, is both goal-oriented and tool-oriented. But if we assume that orientation towards a goal such as livelihood may be impelled by instinct, the orientation of the agent towards tools is not thus instinctually prompted. Ends can be presupposed, while means have to be deliberately planned. The paradoxical position of work here becomes prominent in the sense that work, though an elementary intervention, cannot be separated in the process from deliberate interventions. Here again the distinction between the bodily aspect and the mental one becomes less sharply delineated than is usually assumed. Obviously, we are here suggesting the possibility of the process of a massed accumulation of tools, an accumulation whose primary *raison d'être* lies in tools' functional character. But the dialectics of estrangement may also be massive, and the building of tools will become an end in itself. At this juncture we are referring to the *locus* of technique — and we shall come back to this issue at a subsequent stage of our analysis. In any case, it can be assumed that the more tools are needed for the goal the less direct is the relationship between the organism and the goal, and, together with this, that the presence of the element of programming or planning increases in proportion to the scope of the work.

But it would be one-sided to suppose that the aspect of programming or planning emerges within the scope of work only through the intermediary of tools. The orientation towards the goal and the anticipation of the goal or the results of the work already contain within themselves an element of planning. Planning is an anticipation of a product, and acts are performed deliberately in order to achieve the product or to bring it about. The very spatial and temporal distance between the organism and the products being created to satisfy its needs, as well as the work done towards the creation of these products and the concomitant satisfaction — all these presuppose and involve an attitude towards the future, i.e. the understanding, explicit or not, that reality may respond to the intervention by letting the product emerge and satisfay our expectations, etc. These are acts of planning — they do not totally lack any reference to tools, but they are obviously more goal-oriented than activities whose axes are tools viewed as means. Hence it can be said that planning directed towards the building of tools is an amplification of the planning already present in the very direction toward goals.

(4)

We have to reiterate, before we proceed, the aspect of the approach to reality which is inherent in work — an approach in the sense of being imbued with, explicit or implicit, reflection; at this point, we are perhaps close to what Merleau-Ponty's terms *'practognosis'*. Certain presuppositions are implied in the approach to work, since work is an access to reality guided by the assumption that reality is open or accessible to that access. The openness of reality, which is the presupposition of any act, becomes more pronounced in relation to work, since reality is viewed not only as open in the broad and vague sense of term but is useable or useful. Nature and the materials available in it can be turned into products, accomplished through acts of labour and work, which will serve the worker's expectations and will thus be useful. It is irrelevant whether the usefulness is of a primary character, serving and satisfying a need, or of a secondary character, providing the means for satisfaction, e.g. hay or money. Even when we assume that work is an expression of an innate capacity to move, what is sometimes called *Selbstbewegung*, the very fact that work is teleological, and that the movement is performed for the sake of the product, indicates that a built-in planning and reflection accompany work. The concept or category of usefulness is of course an amplification and elaboration of the position and impact of the product, since usefulness is already an abstract notion and is not confined to the particular product aimed at in the particular act of achievement. A reflection upon reflection is implied, namely, the elaboration of the meaning of the product in its position. The very investment of the product with its satisfying impact is already to some extent an interpretation of the product from the point of view of its fulfilling our expectation or, to use a more abstract term, from the point of view of its functional value. The meaning of the functional value is the following: the product has a function of satisfying the need out of which the movement or the thrust of the act emerged. Since the product has a function, it is interpreted as possessing a value, either because it can be viewed in the context of products — and exchangeability will be related to that context — or, because we value the satisfaction of the need. Hence we value the product which provides the satisfaction or is functionally conditioned by satisfaction. Because of this vector from the need to the product and from the product to the need, we observe that work is not just an outburst of energy, though it certainly calls for energy and presupposes it. Work is not just an effort, since work is of a correlated structure; in different terms it can be said that we attempt to satisfy the need but, by the same token, we wish to find that the effort has been worthwhile and that the product indeed fulfils the expected function. Here again the evaluation of the product, elementary as it may be, is invoked, since we place the product not only in the context of its *causa formalis* and *finalis vis-à-vis* the needs, but also in terms of *causa materialis vis-à-vis* the very activity which serves as a bridge between the need for, and the functional position of, the product. The more complex the situation of work, the more it becomes possible to separate one aspect of the total context from the other and to speak about needs in isolation from efforts and about products in isolation from either. The common theory of alienation of the product is obviously related to the structure of work. Yet that theory tends to interpret the alienation of the product as a historical feature of labour and work, due to particular circumstances within the society and its economic system. It is obvious that historical circumstances lead to an intensification of the isolation of the product from the need by bringing about a growing differentiation in the diversified, multi-faceted structure of work. But historical processes cannot create structures of this sort, related to primary acts, out of nothingness. The structure of work lends itself to historical amplification and exaggeration in turning the alienation of the product into a major feature of contemporary society. Yet that structure, even though exaggerated and amplified, is inherent in the basic features of work; history cannot impose its détours on that basic structure but can only give it additional breadth and force. We shall see presently that an additional aspect of alienation, related to exchangeability of products, is also invested in the very structure of the activity of work. But before taking that step in our line of analysis, we must consider the activity of work and labour in its inter-human context.[2]

Here we must reiterate the distinction between accessibility of reality and accessibility *qua* response. Reality as accessible can be used, since it is presupposed that accessibility amounts to the openness — at least — of some segments of reality to human use or shaping in order to use them. The other human being can also be used, but he is encountered as an intervening being, using reality for his own purposes, namely, for the satisfaction of his needs. He is watched in this capacity and activity of his or, to put it differently, reality as open is not open only to ourselves but to our fellow-man as well. Precisely because work is an intervention in reality, it is by the same token broader than the act of intervention and the purpose the act pursues. Therefore reality is open to more than one act of intervention and, by a kind of induction, it is open not only to one intervener but, similarly, to other interveners.

To some extent the process of recognition of the other man *via* the activity of work is similar to the process of recognition of the other man in and *via* the linguistic expression. We recog-

---

2. Since we have used Aristotelian distinctions in terms of the different causes, it is apposite to mention here that Paul Natorp refers to economic activities as a matter or material of social life, referring to law and the legal system as the form of social life. Yet, we may wonder whether this juxtaposition of matter and form can be applied to the context with which we are concerned. We have seen to what extent cognitive attitudes are inherent in work, let alone in economic activity as related to work and its utilization. Cf. Paul Natorp: *Vorlesungen über praktische Philosophie*, Verlag der Philosophischen Akademie, Erlangen, 1925, pp. 373ff.

nize that somebody — in order to avoid the expression 'something' — is doing what we are doing, and this resembles the situation where somebody is talking as we are. We recognize the similarity of the activity and are forced to become aware that this similarity is not accidental but is grounded in our common position as active as well as talking beings. The similarity or the parallelism can be extended one step further. The talking being is not only talking but is also responding to our talk, as we are responding to his. The active being engaged in work can respond to our invitation to work with us — and it has been said that not only collaboration is working together but competition also is a joint enterprise, though divided in its direction or in its attempt to achieve the same product or results. To be sure, response on the level of work presupposes response on the level of talking. It is immaterial whether or not the talking is explicit or is implied in the situation. The response is based on the assumption that more than one human being is approaching the work, trying to discern the accessibility of reality. Here too the response may be related to the carrying out of the activity, to the bringing about of the product, or to the materialization of both. Once we refer to this inter-human context, we may see the *locus* of one particular shape and direction of that context, namely response as supplementation, that is to say, when one human being as an agent engages in one direction for the sake of a particular product, relying on the other human being's activity and its product to supplement his own activity and its product. At this juncture it is appropriate to analyse this aspect of the responsive situation inherent in the working intervention.

(5)

The inter-human context, amounting to an attitude of response, calls for several distinctions which are significant in our attempt to posit work in its proper context. Within the attitude of response we first find the aspect of differentiation, which is of both an individual and a typical character. Differentiation expresses itself in the distinction of individuals doing certain things and occupying, to say the least, certain positions in space. Response does not obliterate this differentiation which is, on the contrary, presupposed, and the response can only take place against the background of the differentiation. Stated briefly, the other individual does not become myself in and through response. An additional typical component of differentiation, and most probably the first manifestation of that typical differentiation, is the awareness of the difference between men and women. But there is no limit to the typological interpretation of differentiations, and retrospectively we can introduce into that context such typical distinctions as those between carpenter and cobbler when the individual in question, while maintaining his different position, is viewed in his interaction with typical features; or, as is the case in our everyday life, when the individual and his typical function are viewed as coalescing. The attitude or the activity of differentiation serves as a background to the attitude of response which is, as it were, a level established on the basis of differentiation. Response is an attempt to overcome the distance in spite of the existing differentiation, and supplementation in work is one of the main manifestations of that aspect inherent in response. Once I myself become aware of the limited character of my activity, both as an activity as such and in terms of its product, since e.g. the production of a tool is by the same token the non-production of a house, I may look for the supplementation implied in the response of the other human being who is equally aware of the limited character of his activity as well as that of his product. Obviously, the turn or shift from response in general to response *qua* supplementation does not occur automatically. The shift calls for a sort of communication between the working and the producing human beings who concur in establishing the background of supplementation which in turn may become exchangeability: the invested energy or activity and their product are supplemented by, and mutually exchangeable with, the invested energy and product of the other human being. Within the context of supplementation and exchangeability, a sort of planning is implied. This should not surprise us since planning is already implied in the line of activity, work and product. In addition to this, expectation and anticipation are implied because of the distance in time between the work and its product, let alone the satisfaction of needs expected from the product. The distance is not in time but also in space, since the worker realizes that the product is outside him, though the satisfaction of the need will, in some cases, come about when the product is brought back into the orbit of the worker — as is the case with food and clothes. To view the other worker in the nexus of supplementation and exchangeability is therefore not a totally new perspective, once we relate that perspective to the habits of abstraction, anticipation and expectation. We expect that the other worker will concur with the direction of supplementation because he finds himself in the same situation in which I find myself, namely, aware of the limited character of my activity and its product. To be sure, but for communication of a linguistic or non-linguistic character it would hardly be possible to assume the supplementation and the exchangeability. The achievement of these presupposes the possibility of communication which in turn creates a common ground on which supplementation and exchangeability take place, even when that common ground is of a very limited character like expressing a wish, dividing a territory, etc.

But supplementation and exchangeability presuppose an additional awareness which in turn serves as an even broader background for the process. Supplementation takes place not only because we are aware of the fact that the achievement carries a limitation as its correlate — e.g. that food is not cloth and *vice versa*. This awareness further relates to awareness of our needs, which are broader than the possibility of gratification by a limited activity or work, or by the product achieved. We need both food and clothes and look for the satisfaction of these needs, and alas, we are aware of an additional facet, that is, the continuing character of these needs, which can never be satisfied once and for all. The expectation aroused by the needs and their scope and the expectation related to the ongoing character of the drive to satisfy them turn awareness and attention in the direction of supplementation and eventually exchangeability, since both are meant to solve the problems unsolved on the level of needs within the individual scope, in terms of breadth and time. Hence supplementation and exchangeability are related to one of the basic human modes of awareness, which we previously called practicability — connoting in the present context the assertion whether or not it is feasible to expect the full and continuous satisfaction of needs within the individual orbit. That mode of awareness can now be named realizability, that is, the assertion whether the needs giving momentum to the activity of work can eventually find their satisfaction within the scope of the individual sphere of activity.

We find here an interaction between awareness of breadth and continuity and the partialness of our activity and its result. The aspect of supplementation and exchangeability in our concurrence with the other agent or co-worker and his product is therefore an attempt to enlarge the limited scope of achievement inherent in one's individual orbit by bringing in additional shares contributed by the other worker to satisfy the breadth and time-span of our original impelling needs. It is at this juncture that the aspect of economic considerations comes into play, if the economic aspect is broadly understood as related to a decision about the satisfaction of needs. That satisfaction must be fulfilled and safeguarded here and now, but by the same token offers what has been called *Dispositionszeit* (time for disposition), that is, creating the disposition for further drives towards satisfaction and further acts of work.[3] We can expand on this and say that the affinity between work and economic life, as it is called, lies in the rational structure of acts and work, inasmuch as we find in work the scheme of means and ends. That scheme in turn is connected with what is called the problem of scarcity. This has to be said though at this point we do not interpret scarcity as material scarcity but as the limitation inherent in one's work and its products.

Obviously we cannot confine work or labour to that elementary level of satisfying needs which we presuppose as given, or as related to the nature of the organism and its interaction with the surrounding world. The simplest way of putting this is to say that once needs are satisfied, or that there is a warranted expectation that they will be continuously satisfied, we take a step

---

3. Niklas Luhmann: *Soziologische Aufklärung — Aufsätze zur Theorie sozialer Systeme*, Westdeutscher Verlag, 2nd ed., Opladen, 1971; mainly the chapter: 'Wirtschaft als System', pp. 204ff.

in the direction of abstraction related not to the immediate impact of the product but to its shape and quality, and thus engage in an activity which is not prompted only by needs calling for instantaneous satisfaction. We here deliberately maintain the distance between the needs and their satisfaction, though relying on the eventual meeting between the two, and engage in what might be called an activity whose outcome is the refinement of the product and not just the achievement of the product itself. One can, of course, suggest that the time-distance or the deferment of the satisfaction presuppose an 'aesthetic' need. One can suggest that because there is a time-lag there is ample time for additional needs to arise. But we shall not concern ourselves with the questions of priority. It can be maintained that the conception of the interrelation between activity and product can be maintained even when we move beyond the elementary character of work and labour related to the immediate satisfaction of the primary needs.

(6)

Here we must realize again that estrangement or alienation related to labour, work and products is not only a historical phenomenon due to a particular mechanism of a society and its particular structure. Once we engage in exchanges and exchangeability we see the merit of the product and of those who bring it about first of all in their involvement in the process of exchangeability. We do not view the product or the producer in their position within the broad or comprehensive human context. We view them in what we might call proximity with ourselves, amounting here to their actual or expected contribution to our needs, which in turn cannot be satisfied except by implicating our fellow and his product in the texture of our own lives. A paradox is inherent in this description or proximity and exchangeability going together, since proximity is in the first place supplementation. Work as such and the relationship established during and through it, including in the economic sphere, do not justify an evaluation of the other person, except from the point of view of exchangeability. Since exchangeability refers to a commodity, those who provide for exchangeability are also seen from the perspective of exchangeability of a commodity. Within the confines of the structure of work there is no point of view other than that of mutual supplementation of human needs through human beings, or the instrumental evaluation of human beings. When we adopt norms which go beyond the structure of work and the economic orbit, for instance the moral norm, we neutralize to some extent the predominant impact of the norm of work and criticize work by evaluating it according to a norm which is imposed on work and does not emerge out of the structure of work itself. If there is more than one norm, we face the question whether one particular norm should be viewed as superior, or perhaps we will have to admit our simultaneous adherence to different norms, and different structures, despite the possible lack of conformity between them. This notion can be differently expressed by saying that within work and all those activities which follow it the prevailing norm is that of utility; we apply the notion of utility to the products, to the acts which bring them about and to the doers whose acts bring the product into existence. We could say: to evaluate something as useful is indeed a high evaluation. But we still face the question whether that norm is inclusive – let alone superior – or whether there are additional norms, regardless of their position. It goes without saving that in our mode of behaviour money is connected with the economic activity, money being a product or tool *par excellence* for the sake of exchangeability, serving at the same time as an abstract mediator between concrete commodities. The fact that the intermediary position of money is emphasized does not preclude the emergence of a rhythm of turning means into ends which, in this context, amounts to a lack – or suppression – of awareness of the exchangeable character of money in terms of its position, thus turning it into an ultimate product or end.

(7)

At this point it is apposite to deal with the technical aspect of work or with technique in general. In a sense, work as such, as an intervention in reality, is something artificial and thus relates to *techne* or to *ars*, in the original sense of those terms. But a closer look will show that there are many aspects to the relationship between work and art. What is visible in the first place is the element of skill which can be viewed as inherent in the deed itself, when the act is 'just' performed in a way regarded as containing dexterity. This, in turn, can be understood as an expedient act and also as one containing an aspect of 'elegance'. In this sense the technical aspect of work is related not to the product nor to the tools but to the mode of its execution. But this is only one and — perhaps — the most elementary component of technique.

Technique can also be viewed from its functional position, namely, as giving release or relief to the act performed, lessening the burden, as for instance, using a hammer instead of the fist. The introduction of technical devices in this context, and not only the mode of performance as such, becomes prominent. In a sense we move here between work and hardship on the one hand and leisure on the other, introducing technical devices in order to shift from hardship to, at least, some extent of leisure.

A third component enters through the awareness that only with the aid of devices or tools can certain works be performed and lead to achievements — we just cannot mine coal with our bare hands. Here technique amounts to the replacement of the energy invested in work or to the extension of the possibilities inherent in the physical performance by prevailing oneself of certain instruments. Here an intermediary is placed between effort and product; technique contains both the aspect of mediation and the aspect of the product it serves. Sometimes the technical device is not merely an extension of the effort in its physical sense, but a replacement of the former — as is the case with printing as against writing. Printing not only replaces the effort invested in writing, but at the same time allows for a wider distribution of the product. That amplification in turn can be interpreted as efficiency, that is to say, for the sake of distributing the product *qua* information it is more efficient to have it printed than to have it handwritten.

Both work in the basic sense and the various technical devices give rise to a certain amount of knowledge which accompanies them or is sometimes their unintended by-product. When we intervene in nature by sowing grain, even in the most elementary fashion by using our hands, we first assume, as we have seen earlier, that nature or the soil will respond to our act, and we subsequently learn whether or not this anticipation or prediction is realized. We may also learn the relationship between the achievement and, for instance, rain and the cyclical character of the emergence of the product expected. But when we use technical devices, we invest a certain knowledge in their construction and from the construction and its activization we may learn about equilibrium, or laws of motion, and so on. Since the construction already implies a certain method or methodical prediction about the outcome and the fitness of the product constructed, knowledge acquired by the application of the construct is also methodical, or at least less desultory than that acquired through immediate intervention in the soil or in nature. The aspect of utility accompanies the construction as it does labour and work. But constructions are more mediated than the activity of work; thus in a sense constructions are both links and barriers between the actor and his planned achievement. Since this is so, the artifact of technique is in turn a product, and we may work to fashion it, though eventually it will serve the product in terms of its intervention in nature or in the surrounding world. Once constructs are brought into the context, we may sometimes wonder what is their functional position and whether or not they are really needed for the desired product, since they themselves are also products. Here we may encounter an additional level of possible alienation in the sense that we lose sight of the *raison d'être* of the mediators, and the very construction becomes an end in itself. From the economic point of view it can be said that the introduction of the sphere of mediation opens possibilities for competition between different constructs serving the same aim or ultimate product, assuming that the achievement of the product is sufficient motivation for the application of the construct. Thus it can be presupposed that the motivation is there and the competitive strife centers around the mediating constructs.

Because of this situation it is often argued that a certain construct is more suitable for the achievement of the ultimate product, the creation of which is taken for granted as sufficient motivation for the process of intervention. At this point we may suggest a very thin line of demarcation between technique and technology once technique is understood as the sum-total of constructs for predetermined ends, such as products for the alleviation of the burden of work, whilst technology can be understood as the sum-total of products or constructs unrelated to predetermined ends or by themselves creating their own ends. This is of course — as we have said — a very thin line, because technological constructs, like aeroplanes or computers, are still related to certain anticipated ends, like overcoming distances in time and space or the acceleration of a process of counting, extrapolation, etc. But the products or achievements are of a different order compared with the products of labour in the basic sense *qua* intervention in nature for the satisfaction of given and constant needs. Technological constructs in a sense create their own needs, like the need to be in another place as quickly as possible or the need to forecast certain events etc. We can characterize the technological sphere as being simultaneously more abstract and more methodical or even methodological than the sphere of technique. Indeed it is grounded not only in accumulated human experience but in the sciences, in particular natural science, which is obviously of a methodical character. Thus technology can be seen as deliberate intervention in the surrounding world: intervention that starts with work and labour and finds its peak in the technological sphere by being a planned intervention for the sake of producing constructs, methods, as well as newly emerging needs or reshaped needs. It is because of this ongoing character of technology and the salient assumption that it will give rise to needs succeeding the product and not anteceding it, that economic activity related to continuous production and consumption finds a corollary as well as a cluster of motivation in technology.

Winding up this part of our analysis of technique within the scope of work, we can suggest the following aspect of technology as pertinent to our discussion: in the first place, technique appears as a counterpoint of nature, just as work appeared as a counterpoint of reality. It is an attempt to give shape to natural materials or factors by using them or by moulding them, keeping in mind the human needs for whose satisfaction that intervention was undertaken in the first place. In this context one can see the harvest as an artifact, but it is more appropriate to see the harvest brought about by human intervention as remote from the means used for producing it. In a different sense, we distinguish between creative activity, as for instance that of a composer, and performing activity, containing an aspect of skill and technique which, as we have seen, is, broadly speaking, the mode of performance, either inherent in the performer or in the device he uses for the performance. At this point we are already distinguishing between art and technique as 'handwork', referring to machines in contradistinction to creations like pictures, symphonies or novels, although, even with reference to the sphere of art, we sometimes refer to technical characteristics, whether in relation to the work as such or to its presentation. In any case, the reference to technical aspects here becomes removed from the product and refers to the mode of presenting the product or giving it precisely a non-methodical touch, as in the case of a pianist's technique. Summing up, we may say that with all these distinctions, work and labour seem to be of a more immediate character in terms of intervention in reality, while technique is of a more mediated character. The dialectical scale leads us to the observation that technology, like work, again intervenes directly in reality — not so much through the exercise of the mere activity but through the very presence of the construct in reality and in nature.[4]

The aspect of technology will concern us in further contexts.

4. Consult

a. Hannah Arendt: *The Human Condition*, University of Chicago Press, 1958; mainly pp. 79ff.

b. Remy C. Kwant: *Philosophy of Labor*, Duquesne Univ., Pittsburgh; Editions E. Nauwelaerts, Louvain, Belgium, 1960.

The various aspects of alienation are discussed in the article 'Aspects of Identity and Alienation' by the present author in *Interpretation*, 1980, pp. 156-173.

CHAPTER FOUR

DIVERSIFICATION OF ACTION:
HISTORY AND TECHNOLOGY

(1)

Our previous exploration has already introduced the element of technique into the scope of elements relevant to labour and work. The sphere of this discussion was man's attitude to nature as representing or embodying reality. Technique is a kind of intermediary between man and nature since on the one hand it relates to man's given needs and on the other to his intervention in nature for the sake of satisfying these needs through means invented by himself and moulded by the given instruments of work. Nature is the environment while technique is the equipment for facing that environment, going beyond the given instruments but retaining the purpose of fulfilling the functions which the given equipment cannot fulfil by itself.

Yet the relation between man's intentionality and the reality he confronts, together with the complexity of the relations between reflection and action, is not confined to the 'pre-existent' reality and the 'fundamental' approach to it embodied in labour. There are leaps in that interaction, and not only modes of continuity, as Marx, for instance, asserted when he referred to the 'first historical act'. History is created, and continuously so, but is not created by a mere act, but rather by a conjunction of action and anticipation. Actions give rise to events and hence the dictum of *wirksam ist was wirkt* applies to this sphere. Yet in order to identify that which was *wirksam* we need reflection as an approach of looking back at the process or the course of events. Hence it is not accidental that history has two meanings: that of *res gestae* and that of *historia rerum gestarum*, though the meanings can be distinguished verbally rather than structurally. Moreover: 'pre-existent' reality enters the orbit of history when history absorbs, as it were, natural events — which does not imply that the absorption is harmonious, as in the case of an earthquake. The process gives momentum to actions leading to events that are related to nature, like the discovery of a continent; or else the process represented, for instance, by a political structure leads to inventions and their activization, such as the atom bomb. Thus, phenomenologically, history, though created and not pre-existent becomes an environment, in itself not totally detached from nature but not totally submerged in it either. Though it is grounded in action, we discern in history itself the evolvement of a new synthesis. Again, the term 'synthesis' does not imply a pre-established harmony between the elements present in it.

By way of an introductory summary we may add the following comment: as technique is to be regarded as the extension of work on the level of the encounter between man and nature, technology is to be regarded as the embodiment of man's deliberate intervention in reality against the background of history. This relationship between technology and history can retrospectively be called 'historical', that is if we look at technology from the angle of accumulated interpretations in the context of the modern world. Furthermore, technology becomes an order in history and not longer represents scattered interventions in nature or instruments invented for the sake of that intervention. The order is created and as such it has a foothold within the created process of history, giving a certain shape or momentum to that process. The continuity of history is the background for the continuity of technology, which is inherent in the very term 'order'. We shall now go on to analyze this level of intervention of human beings in given reality. The impact of technology on human activity will again be one of our concerns when we come to deal with the structure of political activity.

(2)

Every retrospective analysis starts out from a certain given order, or at least from certain given circumstances. For an analysis of presuppositions of history we must bear in mind that we are conducting that analysis in present age as it is, a present which is so largely shaped by technological momentum and by the order that technology creates and recreates. Obviously, technology itself emerged in history and has its own history. From this point of view we can suggest a term parallel to 'poetic' justice, i.e. 'historic' justice: an order based on intervention and not on interpretation is eventually exposed to interpretation. Technology is related to intervention *qua* manipulation. Hence we become aware of the difference, precisely because of the impact of technology, between interpretation — reflective interpretation— and manipulation as intervention — a deliberate and methodical intervention. From this point of view an analysis of technology may focus our attention on the differences between the technological attitude to time and the historical attitude to it. Our experience of technology may sharpen — or shape — our understanding of history and conversely, our understanding of history may sharpen — or shape — our understanding of technology. This aspect of technology as an order of reality vs. history as a continuous shaping of time through interpretation will be the focus of our present investigation. To this end, we must introduce several distinctions, some of them clearly related to the traditional distinctions between knowledge and *techne* and the different variations on that theme.

Prima facie the common ground of history as a process of actions and events and of technology as intervention in the given order, seems to be obvious. Both realms can be viewed as related to man as an active being, as *homo faber* in the broad sense of the term and as a tool-making animal, though the latter description is usually considered more applicable to the orbit of technology than to that of history. But if we attempt to understand more closely the meaning of the terms involved, and especially the practical aspect of human nature and its manifestation — Marx took this aspect as constitutive of history — we realize how ambiguous all these descriptions are. We shall start a closer examination with an attempt to pinpoint certain aspects implied in the broad concepts or terms.[1]

1. Cf. J. Ellul: *The Technological Society*, transl. J. Wilkinson, New York, Knopf, 1964; and his: "Symbolic functions, technology and society', *Journal of Social Biological Structures*, Vol. 1, No. 3, 1978, pp. 207ff.

Nature can be understood as the sum-total of that which is originally given and present before any human intervention takes place. As against this, technique as we have pointed out, is the sum-total of objects not originally given, implanted as it were into the surroundings of nature and made present by certain modes and ways of handling. Technique connotes not only the objects introduced but also the ways in which they were introduced. For this reason technique cannot be viewed as separate from acts of intervention and thus eventually from the presence of the human beings who are the real causes of the acts of technique. Objects introduced by acts of intervention belong to the sphere of intervention, which is one of the synonyms employed for the purpose of describing the nature of technique. In this context Artistotle's concepts of *techne* or *poiesis* and his description of inventive technique as productive knowledge should be recalled. We sometimes tend to describe the realm of invented objects and the acts leading to intervention as the realm of artificiality, the latter being contrasted with nature as the sum-total of objects originally present. However, within the realm of things and ways made present or created, the classical distinction between *praxis* and *poiesis* has to be recalled: *praxis* is related to will whereas *poiesis* is related to skill. For the sake of our present analysis, we may leave out the aspect of will, though it inheres in action, and confine ourselves to the aspect of skill. Following the classical description we understand skill as the power of faculty of engendering things or of ways of handling them. Here, too, the classical description of technique as embracing objects and modes of handling them returns: we stress the aspect of skill as engendering things on the one hand and the aspect of products on the other.

(3)

The bridge between te realm of nature and the realm of artificiality seems to be provided by the concept of human needs; hence we have already considered technique in the context of work. Technique takes advantage of nature and its objects for the sake of satisfying human needs. The need for shelter, for instance, is satisfied by building houses of raw material found in nature; or else structures in nature and potentialities inherent in it are used, e.g. vegetation being made available by exploiting the rhythm of nature for the sake of human needs. What underlies this interpretation is an attempt to point to a line of continuity from nature to artificiality: according to that description there is bound to be a *ratio essendi* for the artificial object — and that *ratio* is not itself artificial. The concept of human needs refers to data preceding the establishment of objects whose final purpose is the satisfaction of those needs. At this point we again refer to Marx's interpretation of history, namely, that the process of satisfaction of human needs, which is in a sense a technical process, is by the same token a historical process: only through involvement in actions and processes can human needs be met and expectation and satisfaction can factually occur.

The historical aspects come to the fore in an additional consideration, namely, that techniques, as modes of handling the response to needs, change in the course of time and, as we shall see, needs, though primarily given, also do not remain separated from the processes aimed at their satisfaction. To some extent, at least, they change along with the processes of this satisfaction and perhaps more than change if new needs emerge. In addition, there is a link between the technical and the historical aspects when we refer to the medium intervening between needs and the outcome of processes *qua* satisfaction. That medium is an understanding of the needs by way of reflecting on them and initiating through reflection devices for their satisfaction. Further still, an aspect of anticipation through reflection is present, that is to say, the actual products to come are expected to satisfy the needs. One may conjecture at this point that these different components of reflection present in the technical process led Aristotle to list *techne* under the heading of knowledge and not only under the heading of skill. The same argument applies to history. At this juncture it can already be said: the historical process is broader than the technical, as reality of modes of intervention, not only skills, as well as a variety of products like institutions and the public sphere in general, and not only tools, gadgets and other varieties of modes of satisfying needs. To be sure, it is easier to separate off the aspect of human needs underlying the technological process than to separate off one layer of human existence as serving as an efficient cause of the historical process. This too is due to the difference between the manifoldness of reality and the contraction inherent in any mode of intervention, be it as sophisticated as it may.

A paradoxical conclusion emerges from this comparison: the coalescence of the historical process with the technical, and the juxtaposition between the two insofar as both processes are related to the same outcome. Although technique is aimed towards products, established for the sake of already existing human needs, these products can be detached from the producer. This is so because technique, at least partially, is embodied in both material products and objective ones, such as organizations as defined or delineated modes of co-existence. To the extent that history is not manifested in material products — which are of a technical character — its objective products, though not totally immersed in the producers, are still not totally alienated from them. A parliamentary institution or a legal system in which actual human beings do not live and operate ceases to be an actual historical institution and becomes a vestige or a documentary relic. The actual and active interaction between the producer and the product is a feature of the historical process, though not necessarily a feature of the technical one. It is perhaps no accident that Marx, who in a way took the technological rhythm as epitomizing the historical process, also took alienation of the product from the producer as a paradigm of his analysis and evaluation of the historical process as a whole, viewing alienation as a total historical phenomenon and not only as a phenomenon within the orbit of technology. In addition it can be said that, since it is more plausible to extract from the technological process one singular driving force, namely, the satisfaction of human needs, the question of a teleological evaluation of the technical order is more plausible than a teleological evaluation of the historical process and order. There is a built-in *telos* to technique; hence we can ask whether or not that *telos* is actually achieved, or whether or not an additional *telos* has been superimposed on the primary *telos* as, for instance, the domination of the world — an aspect comprised under the heading of what Max Scheler called dominating knowledge (*Beherrschungswissen*).

(4)

Technology as it has developed is more than a sum-total of scattered skills and disconnected products. It is what Ellul calls an ensemble: the status of an order or of reality, of a self-sufficient reality with its own special laws and its own determinations is thus conferred on technology. To be sure, when we speak of technology as an order of reality, we may still vacillate between a view which refers to technology as an ensemble of means — thus clinging to the original meaning of technique as the sum-total of products aimed at satisfying human needs — and a view which conceives of technology as a sphere of reality which is no longer a domain of means or an intermediary domain and whose *ratio essendi* lies in itself. This position can be viewed as a reinforcement of the aspect of alienation: we may hesitate to ask what is the purpose of nature, though we will ask what is the purpose of artificially introduced objects is, precisely because they have been artificially introduced. Once we cease to ask questions about the purpose of artificiality we, surreptitiously, bestow the status of nature on the orbit of artificiality. Alienation becomes not only an expression of a human response: it is established and thus possesses a new status. One of the most common criticisms of technology is related to the aspect of alienation, since we do not, after all, lose sight of the artificial aspect implied in technology. Thus, we do not totally reject the evaluation of technology according to its presupposed or taken-for-granted *raison d'être* or *telos*. Moreover, with the increased impact of technological products or of the technological order on human life, when human existence echoes, as it were, the rhythm of the technological order, the line of demarcation between what is humanly internal and external becomes blurred. At this point we can say that the technological order, as it has developed, has become a major historical event: it prescribes actual human relations taking place in time as it channels human drives in the direction of what goes by the name of rising expectations, improving standards of living, etc. Technology thus seen ceases to be only one of the channels of human activity within the broad orbit of history. It becomes a focus of human activity, expressed in various and different parallel channels of that activity. Thus, as a matter of fact, we may trace not only the impact of technology on our behaviour as consumer, or producer, in the economic province, but also the impact of technological media on the democratic process. Technology has changed, for instance, the relations between voters and candidates, making the candidates visible in the medium of television and thus, as it were, present in the *agora* and not kept remote by the different intermediary devices of institutional or democratic procedures. We can enlarge on this by saying that technology has introduced into historical consciousness the presentness not only of objects but also of events and people. It has reduced distances and along with this has contracted the scope of anticipation. Since the technological rhythm creates repercussions in the accelerated rhythm of historical consciousness as a whole, the paradox of technology lies in that, together with widening the horizons of space, it has brought about the contraction of the horizons of time. It has an impact on the historical process and the awareness of it despite the fact that it is itself an historical event or a continuous chain of events. This is to show that the dialectic of the total process, i.e. history, and the partialness of another process, i.e. technology, cannot simply be understood as leading in the direction from the total to the partial. The partial, once established and significant, has its feedback to the total. This interaction also implies a complicated structure of relations between reflection and action.

(5)

It is apposite to pay attention to the impact of the technological structure on the historical consciousness, precisely since the present analysis is not oblivious of the impact of the *Zeitgeist* on the direction and dimensions of the historical consciousness. The

first point to be made in this context is that historical consciousness, though it refers simultaneously to the past and to the future,
has as its starting point that which is given in the present. It has
to be explained through the past and is the locus of the intentionality towards the future. The to-be-explained present is thus
regarded as an object for explanation and the given circumstances for the step forward. Technological intervention is obviously non-explanatory; it is mainly directed towards the future.
It does not anticipate the future as a dimension: in a sense it
creates that which will exist in the future, at least within the
confines of instruments and the order to be established by them.
While historical consciousness takes the present as the given, the
technological attitude is inclined to take within its orbit the
given present as equivalent to the obsolete which has to be replaced by instruments, to be established in the future or operate
in it, or by the embracing order which will have as its justification an improvement of the present order — whatever 'improvement' may mean. Hence technological intervention presupposes
or contains in itself the evaluation of the given according to its
significance, when gauged by the standard of instrumentality,
whilst historical consciousness implies the evaluation of the given
as calling for exploration.

This can be put differently: intentionality towards the future,
characteristic of technological intervention, aims at improvement
and perfection of the instrument; thus the technological replacement is a deliberate act aiming at improvement. Whereas the
historical consciousness considers replacement as concomitant
with the very transition in and of time and cannot derive the
tendency towards perfection merely from the reading of the
data. The historical consciousness *accepts* the datum of the
change, while the technological attitude deliberately *introduces*
change. It is because of this difference that in a predominantly
technological civilization we experience what can be called the
accelerated pace of change, a pace which is due to the rhythm
of the technological innovations as well as to the impact those
innovations have, directly or indirectly, on historical consciousness in general and on the immanent rhythm of time of that
consciousness. In this sense the *Zeitgeist* of our era can be described not only through the presentness of the technological

rhythm in total configuration, but also by turning the technological rhythm into a paradigm for the diversity of rhythms in
the historical process, or by making that rhythm the most predominant factor in the total historical configuration.

Further still: historical consciousness, being related to the
three dimensions of the present turning to the past and anticipating the future, has its built-in limitation in this three-fold
structure. The technological attitude is future-oriented and considers — if we can attribute 'consideration' to it — the future
not only as the relevant dimension but the only one of significance. This is so because the future represents the open horizon
and as a result the technological attitude lacks a paradigm controlling and guiding it.[2] There are no paradigms but only instruments involved in a continuous process of replacement. The
openness of the future and the absence of a guiding principle or
idea are, therefore, interrelated. The impact of that attitude on
historical consciousness is far-reaching, since historical conscious-
nees, out of its own resources, can discern different historical
layers or traces of different historical periods as concurrently
present in a configuration. The ancient can be present and is not
replaced, let alone removed. What is ancient for historical consciousness is obsolete for the technological attitude.

Yet, historical consciousness, though somehow shaken or
undermined by the technological attitude, can still hold its own.
This is so since it presents a broad spectrum of orders of reality
and thus puts forward co-ordinates for comparison — and a comparison is in a sense a mode of mitigation. Let us take as an
example one of the prevailing criticisms of technology as related
to alienation, which we have already mentioned. In a way,
alienation is inescapable in any order of reality created by
human efforts; technology is no exception. Any order has to be
looked at simultaneously from two points of view: as being
created by the producer or producers and as being independent
of him or them. From this point of view the tension, or the
doom, of the order of technology resembles the order of state-

2. This connotation probably underlies the title and the main argument of Denys
Gabor's *Inventing the Future*, Harmondsworth, Penguin Books, 1963.

hood, and even the order of laguage as well. This lesson is brought home by a comparison which in turn implies a historical comparison. The very fact, to take the example of language, that we express our impressions in words makes words, at least, semi-independent of our impressions: words, as such, are not created by our immediate impressions. The impressions, as it were, find their way to the words and with them to the order of language. In a sense the creator cannot be self-sufficient since his self-sufficiency would amount to self-enclosure, to silence and even to more than silence, to a lack of an internal or inner articulation. Only when we accept Bergson's assumption that thought and language remain incommensurable can we assume that the creative act and the order are bound to be totally estranged by their very definition and not by the consequences or repercussions of the order.[3]

To assume such an incommensurability presupposes an even more fundamental incommensurability: between what Bergson called true feeling, which is a continual becoming, and the unchanging external objects, and still more the incommensurability between the feeling and the word. Historical consciousness serves here as the corrective consciousness against so many attempts to see processes as either confined to the pole of 'true' feeling or as confined to the pole of independent orders. Once we realize that historical creations contain in themselves actions or perpetual human enterprises directed to institutions and orders, as well as orders which, in turn, like institutions, are events and thus situations or contexts, we realize that technology from the point of view of historical consciousness has to be seen as *one* of the orders. We realize this even when we grant the predominance of technology in a certain historical situation. We have to distinguish here between a structural criticism which incorporates the criticized order in a spectrum of orders, according to the lesson of history, and a romantic criticism which removes the historical perspective and contents itself with the duality and tension between 'true' feelings and orders.

---

3. Henry Bergson: *La Perception du Changement, Conferences faites à l'Université d'Oxford*, The Clarendon Press, Oxford, 1911.

(6)

The analogy between technology as an order and the orders which were traditionally the subject matter of historical awareness may lead to an additional conclusion with reference to human subjects and their reflections, in their various modes.

There exists a correlation between the respective spheres, i.e. space and time, and the attitudes directed toward them. The sphere of time is by definition a sphere of change, or to use the Kantian term it is the form of succession. Hence change or changes are initially given: historical existence and historical consciousness are involved in investing the changes that occur with meanings, not because of history but because of the time component of reality. Space is initially a form of co-existence and not of change, or, put differently, changes cannot be presupposed as data for an attitude directed towards space. Changes have to be deliberately introduced into the sphere of space; hence the technological approach to reality is not one of endowing reality with meanings, but one of controlling reality: either controlling it by taking advantage of the laws of nature pertaining to reality — and we shall refer to this component of the technological attitude presently — or by introducing instruments into the scope or reality, designing them and directing them toward defined or delineated purposes.[4]

As history presupposes time and succession, so technology, with all its refinements, presupposes the laws of nature and is subservient to them; obviously it does not create them. To be sure, a change, or even a rupture as it is sometimes called, has occurred in this area: what can be described as pre-modern technology — and this is technique rather than technology — took advantage mainly of materials found in nature and used or utilized them through the technical medium for certain purposes. Modern technology tends rather to take advantage of the science of nature, that is to say of laws of nature, as distinguished from

4. J. Dewey: *The Quest for Certainty, A Study of the Relation of Knowledge and Action*, London, Allen and Unwin, 1930, p. 234.

materials supplied by it. In modern technology, therefore, compared with the preceding stages of technical developments, we can discern a shift from the material stratum to the structural one. This shift expresses itself not only in the invention of materials or their recycling, but in the designing of instruments whose instrumentality relates mainly to the fact that they comply with the laws of nature and as such can serve as instruments for the prescribed purposes. Yet this statement implies an additional paradoxical, or even dialectical, aspect of the technological order. Here, too, we realize the difference between the historical process and the technological orbit: though technology presupposes the structural, i.e. the causal character of nature and reality, it imposes objectives on that structure. Technology is inherently teleologically oriented and that orientation leads to the utilization of the causal rhythm of reality. The teleological aspect is present even when we cannot – or do not want – to identify the objectives of the technological creations as responding to human needs. The technological order as it develops is pushed forward by its own momentum. Thus perpetual change becomes a feature of that order or its objective. From this point of view modern technology resembles an aspect implied in Kant's description of an object of art: it is teleological without having a *telos*, it has finality without having an end outside itself.[5] The teleological character can be genetically related to the momentum of responding to human needs. But it can also be related, from the point of view of the structure of the technological situation, to the predominance of the dimension of the future – the predominance we referred to in the preceding part of our discussion. To move in the direction of the future without any material or substantive *telos* involved in the horizon of the future adds to the teleological order: its propensity to perpetual change. This aspect of the order can sometimes be characterized as bringing about change for the sake of change. It can also be understood why a teleological order though it lacks an end may evoke responses or reactions expressed in

---

5. I. Kant: *Kritik d. Urteilskraft*, Akad. Ausgabe, Bd. V, para. 10, p. 220, Meredith, transl. Clarendon Press, Oxford, 1964, p. 61.

statements like 'it is terrifying' or 'anti-rational' in spite of the rationality underlying technology — that rationality which is the concomitant of reliance on laws of nature. These components of the technological order, related to tis 'imposed' structure on the pre-existent structure of reality, have an impact on human society, including political activity. These aspects will be explored presently in the context of the various ingredients of the sphere of politics.

One of the characterisations of technology — and *pari passu* of blames raised against it — is that it creates needs artificially and thus ceases to satisfy primary needs or 'natural' rights. In a way this criticism is warranted. But here, too, historical awareness leads us in the direction of a supplementary evaluation of the impact of technology, an evaluation which again is a lesson history teaches us. The order as such creates its respective responses, but it is not simply created by the primary or motivating needs or impulses. It can be said, coming back to that example, that language and words have their own semi-independent rhythm: they not only express feelings and impressions, but they also evoke sentiments and impressions. Language creates its own resonance and is not only the resonance of given feelings. The same can be said about institutions: they create modes of behaviour and reaction; they mediate primary impulses. To quote a drastic example: one is called upon not to take vengeance when one encounters a criminal act but to postpone or defer one's reaction for the sake of mediation epitomized in the notion or 'the due process of law'. To sum up: orders are expressive but are also formative; criticism, if any, has to be directed against the substance of the formation and not against the position of the formation — and this conclusion applies to technology, in spite of our 'romantic' trend in the prevalent criticism of it.

(7)

We may move now to a further exploration of the position of technology within the domain of history. In so far as technology comprises tools, it fills the space of the world with objects which were not originally present in nature or in space. To put it differently, technology makes space 'denser' than it was in its primary state. Underlying technology is therefore the direction towards the release of human existence, partial indeed, from the environing world as the sum-total of objects, by adding objects to those already present or given. Technology is thus an expansion of human existence within the orbit of objects, i.e. space. *Mutatis mutandis*, the same can be said about history, in terms of time and not of space. History as the open sum-total of creations of the public domain, composed of relations and institutions, fills time by continuously adding contents and factors to those which are already in time. To be sure, to add in time is also to restore or to recapitulate that which already has been created, since the given or already created has to be invested with a meaning in order to be present within the historical awareness. Technological creativity implies the release from that which is already given, while historical creativity, too, is a release from that which is already given by not relying on the primacy succession of occurrences in nature. The bifurcation between history and technology, including the evaluative aspect implied in it, namely the retaining character of historical consciousness and the innovative character of technology, presupposes common human essence. That essence can be characterized as the release from the given, a release which originates from within, from the human propensity, and not from the encountered order of time and space — and in that release we again discern the interrelation between reflection and action.

Having said this, we have to point out what can be described as the superiority or at least primacy of history versus technology, not because of the component of history proper but because of the time component. It is time which bestows its position on history. Filling space through technological devices is a continuous series of actions occupying a position in time, whilst historical awareness is related to the past and the future for the present as such lacks a spatial dimension. It has a spatial dimension because human beings entertaining historical consciousness exist in space and their creations are lodged in it. Yet the creation of human relations between generations, as well as human institutions, the absorption of customs and traditions, the conduct of institutions like legal systems or codes of language etc. are, as such, not placed in space; all these occur in time. From this point of view the historical process is broader than the technological one — and time is more comprehensive than space. Granting Ellul's statement that technical modalities cannot tolerate subjectivity, we have to re-emphasize that they are bound to tolerate 'subjectness', that is to say the status of human responses and the involvement in historical consciousness which, by definition, contains a difference between reality and intervention, in spite of the fact that in a way history as compared with nature is also an intervention.

(8)

We have here another manifestation of a paradox or a dialectic: technology, which is related to the laws of nature, is teleological, while history which is in the fist place circumscribed within the human sphere is not teleological. It cannot be teleological because history as the process of deeds and interpreting them by reflection is the meeting ground between time and meaning; this meeting ground is partial or piecemeal. History is a process of giving meaning to time, which already has a meaning of its own. Thus we cannot characterize history as a superimposition of an aspect of meaning, like instrumentality, on a substratum which can not only be interpreted but also controlled. Since technology introduces an order, it can be essentially teleological; since history reshapes orders, the process of reshaping is multi-faceted. Again, the teleological character of the technological order in a certain sense invites a criticism, since anything which is invented can be faced with the question: *cui bono*? In a sense, one can compare the evaluation of the created order with trends evaluating, e.g. literature, from the point of view of moral purpose or impact, such as are known from Plato to Tolstoy. But an order which is not deliberately created and thus lacks the character of a primary teleology is less prone to be gauged according to a single standard. Again, the artificial can be evaluated according to a standard, while the given in a certain sense has to be taken for granted and consented to. Hence technology invites or evokes evaluation, while history invites or evokes − primarily − assent, or at least an attitude of 'can't help it'.

The teleology without *telos* which is one of the essential features of the technological order in its modern stage calls for a reformulation of that structure. The distinction between means and ends which is the concomitant of the distinction between needs and instruments intended to respond to them, has changed with modern technology. Technological objects are no longer extensions of natural organs, like hands, and are not usually created or established through the intervention of touch. Technological objects are rather created by other objects, that is to say, by other tools. Machines are established by machines; the existence of machines is a precondition for the ongoing process of technological creativity. One can look at this rhythm as an additional example of what goes by the common name of alienation.

To be sure, it is not an alienation from human essence but rather from nature in the primary sense of term, or from the natural equipment of human beings and their bodily posture. Technology acquires the rhythm of mediation within its own confines. Again there is a shift, characteristic of technology, from preconditions built-in in human organs to what may roughly be described as human needs in the historical sense − for instance, needs related to the changes and refinements involved and brought about by the historical process. Somewhere in the background the needs for food, shelter and clothing still loom large. But these needs undergo continuous reshaping in history and in the economic processes. Technology responds here more to the refinements of needs as they appear in the historical process than to the bare needs as they are related to the organism in its biochemic constitution. This is an illuminating, somewhat *post factum*, process of bringing together the historical current of events and technological instrumentality. Hence technology changes not only through its own momentum according to the rhythm of teleology without *telos*, but also through the response expected from it by human beings existing in historical time and operating in the changing circumstances of historical reality. The historical human beings are the consumers and producers and they place the technological order within that scope as an instrument for consumption and production.

Co-extensive with the teleological facet of the technological order, as against the multi-faceted historical process, it is at least possible to ask whether an overall principle or principles of the technological order exist. Here, too, let us recall, for the sake of comparison, that we can point to several principles of the natural order as given, and as such it presents a point of departure for any subsequent distinction between the given and the created, the primary and the secondary, or the natural and the artificial. The natural order as given is also the comprehensive order, that is to say, whatever occurs, including that which is artificially introduced, takes place in all-embracing time and space. This, in a sense, amounts to the primacy of the given, since the given absorbs in itself, or incorporates into its own order, that which is created. The contrary, however, is not true. Ecological problems would not exist were it not for the simple fact that created objects and their manifestations have an impact on the natural order. Hence the separation between the natural and the artificial cannot make the artificial totally self-enclosed and separated from the natural. It is because of the primacy of the natural that we realize in a parallel way that history is also the locus of technological innovations, and, to make a trivial point, technology has its own history, while history as a process does not have its own technology.

(9)

Two overriding principles governing the technological order have to be assumed. We distinguish here between the principles and the rhythms of the process. One principle is that of efficiency, and the other is that of rationality. Sometimes the two principles overlap, but, to some extent at least, they can be analytically distinguished. These principles refer to action but as principles they are of the essence of action.

It has to be stated at the outset that the term 'efficiency', though widely used, is rather ambiguous. Efficiency in the broad sense connotes the facility or power to create effects and products and, more specifically, to bring about success and to proceed fittingly in order to achieve success or a prescribed aim. That term originates in Aristotle in the notion of the efficient cause, as the Latin rendering has it, and it appears, among other contexts in political discourse. John Stuart Mill, for instance, refers to the greatest dissemination of power consistent with efficiency.[6] It can be said that the concept of efficiency, as it became widespread, refers to the aspect of output and results; it is this aspect which made it applicable to engineering in the nineteenth century and to economics in the twentieth. Since the term has absorbed an economic meaning, it connotes a 'reasonable' proportion between the effort invested in an operation and the results achieved. Yet because the term 'reasonable' is ambiguous, the more specific meaning depends upon the particular context. In the field of economic activity we may refer to the capital investment and the interest which the capital yields. Once transposed to the broad organizational orbit, concern with efficiency may be manifested in two different ways: in the political sphere the emphasis may be placed on the maximum participation of people in the enterprise at stake, namely political processes and decisions. A different aspect would come to the fore if we consider an attempt to impose an economic standard on an organization; in this case it can be said with a great deal of justification that maximal results may sometimes be achieved by the minimum participation of a minimum number of people.

The application of the notion of efficiency to the technological order is warranted, since technology is concerned with ends or results. These can be evaluated with reference to the effort invested in them, or the results can be compared with the effort. This is a plausible approach once we are concerned with the technological activity in the self-contained orbit. But as soon as we enlarge the scope of our considerations and introduce a certain economic or social concern, we may come to the conclusion that efficiency conceived in this manner may lead, for instance, to unemployment; unemployment in turn

---

6. J.S. Mill: On Liberty, in *On Liberty and Considerations on Representative Government*, ed. R.B. McCallum, Oxford, Blackwell, 1964, p. 102

would clash with technological efficiency even when economic efficiency would coalesce with technological. Ellul, for instance, refers to efficiency, describing it as that technique which must be applicable without raising storms of protest. It is clear that this definition or description of efficiency shifts from the technological concern to the social, since storms of protest, even when they are iconoclastic or perhaps even Luddite, carry a meaning in the social context and not in the limited technological one. Here again the historical consciousness as comprising a spectrum of activities and their results can serve in the first place as a mitigating factor, once the technological efficiency in the limited sense is put forward. The technological consideration here faces the admonition implied in the historical consciousness or in its lesson.

(10)

Once we look again at the basic factors of technology by tracing them to their efficient causes in the human condition, namely in the continuous drive towards easing human burdens by way of producing tools, machines, etc., as well as taking into account the urge toward dominating the given order of nature and making that order subservient to human goals — we encounter an efficient cause. At the same time we face the question of the human price paid in the achievement of those goals. The two trends, that of lightening the burden and dominating nature, sometimes coincide, as for instance in improving crops. Sometimes they do not coincide, as is the case in military or strategic technology, where the trend toward domination receives priority over the trend toward lightening the burden, though the latter is not totally absent. Sophisticated technology, for example (an example which is trivial), replaces fist-fight. But the order of magnitude of the technology, is such that the concern ceases to be replacement of bodily human effort: the trend toward domination looms central. We realize that the broad human or historical context leads us to the conclusion that there is no unequivocal efficiency, or, to put it differently, there is no monopolistic or exclusive meaning to efficiency which either subsumes the variety of meanings under one meaning or makes one meaning central. To make one meaning of efficiency central presupposes a human i.e. historical decision or context and cannot be attributed to the technological order alone.

To refer again to Ellul, one also speaks about the calculus of efficiency, emphasizing that the search for efficiency is no longer personal, experimental or workmanlike. It is abstract or mathematical and industrial. This meaning of efficiency places it close to the second principle of technology, namely rationality. Rationality, in its broad sense, is an attitude or an activity based on reason. In a more limited sense it is an activity characterized by a methodical structure. It is correlated with the attempt to control the environment or to introduce changes into the through that control. Rationality does not mean rationalism; on the contrary, science has its experiential dimension, though that dimension appears mainly as experimentation, which can be described as controlled experience or experience produced methodically with the view of achieving results which will be methodically warranted. Applied to the technological order, rationality is sometimes presented as a systematic overview of activities or, to look at it from the other end, as division of labour and as application of standards to work and to results. The emphasis is placed on the organization of the activity; once the aspect of organization is introduced, it excludes spontaneity and personal creativity where the two imply human operations and expressions not guided by a method. The organizational and the methodical aspects of technology are two sides of the same coin, since organization implies the removal of the activity from the given and thus from the spontaneous origins of human attitudes and approaches to reality. The affinity between rationality understood in this sense and the analytical aspect inherent in a method can be clearly seen when we recall Descartes' description of what he calls the second precept of his method, namely to divide up each difficulty into as many parts as possible.[7]

7. R. Descartes: *Discourse on Method of Rightly Conducting the Reason, The Philosophical Works*, Vol. 1 (E.S. Halane & G.R.T. Ross, Transl.). New York, Dover, 1933, p. 92.

As a matter of fact, in the organizational and the methodical components of technology we encounter a merger of the two elements characteristic of modern science. As against Descartes and his emphasis on analysis we must remind ourselves of Bacon's saying that no confidence should be placed in the native and spontaneous process of the mind.[8] To be sure, the analysis by dividing up difficulties into as many parts as possible is not spontaneously given; it has to be accomplished through a method, and thus, by definition, it goes beyond the spontaneous equipment of the mind. We can sum up by saying that the technological order as an order deliberately created is a rational order by definition. The historical process embraces in its scope all, or at least a multitude, of human creations and among them the creation of the rational order in the sense described. History appears as an order broader and more absorbing than the technological. Modern technology can be regarded as a partial embodiment of the methodical concept of reason, once reason is not understood the way Plato and Aristotle understood it, namely as a medium of penetration and interpretation of that which is in itself meaningful and ordered, but as a creation of an order through a method. There is a difference between the amorphous historical context and the organized technological order, and probably one of the attractions of technology lies in its organized character. But the organized aspect, looked at more closely, appears essentially as one line of activity which cannot pretend to be superior to the breadth and width of the historical context, neither can it be separated from the latter in spite of the acknowledgement of the different rhythms characteristic of the different orders.

In terms of our concern we notice that rationality grounded in reason and reflection as the latter's activity inheres in the technological order more than in the historical process. History here represents the level of reality while technology embodies the level of a created order — and there is more affinity between rationality and creation than between rationality and reality. Obviously rationality here undergoes a transmutation or contraction.

8. This is the gist of the first part of Bacon's *Novum Organon*.

It is no longer grounded in understanding and manifesting it. It is by definition related to a pursued end — with all the reservations mentioned before as to teleology without *telos*.

(11)

An additional comment is apposite at this point since the term 'pragmatic' appears both in the historical context and in the technological one. The chronological priority is obviously with the historical consideration, since the employment of the term can be traced to Polybius. The 'pragmatic' consideration of history amounts to the exploration of causes and their consequences or effects. To be sure, the introduction of the term 'pragmatic' into the historical context entails the stress that accidental circumstances or secondary details are omitted from pragmatic considerations. In this sense the notion of 'pragmatic' in the historical awareness has an innuendo of strictness or emphasizes concern with the significant or the primary. The technological attitude, by its very definition, is not of an exploratory character; it has a momentum towards control, that is to say, towards production of effects.

It is probably not accidental that there is an affinity between the technological attitude and the pragmatist interpretation in the sense which became widespread and well known in pragmatism as a school of thought. If we refer to William James's simile of keeping our feet upon the proper trail, we refer to an attitude which contains the implication of moving forward and doing so properly, that is to say, methodically, for the sake of results which are not only effects of causes but achievements. We encounter here the variety of meanings of 'pragmatic', and awareness of that variety can lead us to the conclusion that both meanings are justifiably applied in different contexts. The emphasis on the width of the historical context attributes superiority to that context precisely because of its width but not because of the superiority of one of the meanings implied in that context. Technology, as separated from the context, in spite of the fact that it eventually comes back into it, can be viewed from the perspective of a pragmatist consideration. Moreover, we are probably bound to view it from that perspective, once we distinguish between effects and results in a broad neutral sense and those in the technological sense.[9]

We have introduced the issue of history and technology into our exploration in order to exemplify at least partially that the attribution of primacy to reflection over action does not negate the complexity of the relationship between the two attitudes. In a sense the component of action is dominant in both history and technology. But action alone cannot give an adequate account of the two orders. We have considered the order of history as to be listed more with reality than is the order of technology. This difference can perhaps be summed up by saying that history as such is a reality while technology has an impact on reality. However, we must yet consider some more specific modes of activity in order to discern in them the interrelation between reflection and action.

9. Cf. D. Boorstin: *The Republic of Technology, Reflections on Our Future Community*, New York, Harper & Row, 1978.

The present author's *Theory and Practice, An Essay on Human Intentionalities* deals with some aspects of technology, pp. 206ff. The Hague, Martinus Nijhoff.

Eugen Fink in *Traktat über die Gewalt des Menschen*, Vittorio Klostermann, Frankfurt a/M presents a significant analysis of the topic.

CHAPTER FIVE

PLAYING

(1)

In the first place we must explain why we use the term 'playing' as a title for this part of our analysis. We are here following Irving Goffman — to whom we shall frequently refer — who says: 'In the literature on games, a distinction is made between a *game*, defined as a body of rules associated with the lore regarding good starting, and a *play*, defined as any particular instance of a given game being played from beginning to end. *Playing* could then be defined as the process of move-taking through which a given play is initiated and eventually completed; action is involved, but only the strictly game-relevant aspects of action.'[1] Attempting to integrate this distinction into the texture of our argument, it will become clear that we are focussing on action or on activity, though, as will emerge, there is no action without a meaning or, in the case before us, without rules.

We must make a second observation by way of a preliminary outline of the special character of play *vis-à-vis* activity as it is embodied in labour, since we began with labour, and labour as an activity is to some extent a paradigm for other models of activity. If labour is taken to mean the expenditure of time and effort as such, as Max Weber sometimes had it,[2] then every activity can be conceived as labour since every activity takes place in time and involves effort which we sometimes describe as energy or movement. But we have seen in our preceding analysis

---

1. 'Fun in Games', included in *Encounter — Two Studies in the Sociology of Interaction* by Irving Goffman, The Bobbs-Merill Company, New York, 1966, p. 35.

2. *The Theory of Social and Economic Organic Organization* by Max Weber, translated by A.R. Henderson and Talcott Parsons, William Hodge & Co., London/Edinburgh/Glasgow, 1947, p. 202.

that this elementary description certainly does not do justice to the complexities of labour, and therefore, labour proper has to be described by applying more limiting concepts. As is well known, Weber himself referred to utilities (*Nutzleistungen*) which, in his description, are related to the process from means to ends.[3] Again, we have to keep in mind that Weber emphasized the social character of action, which implies an attitude to other human beings; according to him, that attitude is present in labour and concomitantly is bound to be present in other modes of activity, including playing. Certainly, we shall find in the activity of playing an inter-human aspect. But we must ask to what extent that inter-human aspect should be seen as essential and constitutive of every activity, or whether it is only one of the manifestations of that activity. We have seen in our preceding analysis that the inter-human aspect of labour comes to the forefront from the point of view of supplementation and the subsequent concurring, implying division as well as competition. But it is perhaps doubtful whether the activities with which we are concerned — unlike, for instance, the political activity — are to be viewed primarily as implying human interaction or rather human intervention in the surrounding environment, in which the inter-personal or social aspect follows, as it were, the logic or structure of intervention but does not define it from the outset.

(2)

After making these two initial comments, let us go on to our analysis of the activity of playing. Here we encounter several aspects, relying initally on the vague human experience. Playing is usually understood as an exercise or movement, but that exercise lacks a functional or teleological character. Sometimes this free character of movement or movements is understood as simply expressing, for instance, the intrinsic capacity of the body, stretching, exercising, etc. In this sense the activity of playing, lacking an end beyond itself, is also considered to be a

3. *Ibid.*, p. 151.

source of delight and thus related to what goes by the name of 'fun'. Goffman says that games can be fun to play, and fun alone is the approved reason for playing them.[4] Here fun is posited from two angles: as a reason, or thus as an end, of the activity of playing, and as a concomitant resonance of that activity. According to the first interpretation there is indeed a purpose to play. Yet it does not amount to an intervention in the real world but to an enjoyment of one's own activity without evoking the response related to the interaction between, for instance, the product and the need gratified or satisfied. In this sense playing is understood as a pastime activity, or, put differently, the very involvement in the passage of time and giving it a certain direction evokes amusement; it gives us fun. Incidentally, in Hebrew the word for playing, 'siheq', is both in etymology and meaning close to 'zehoq' which means laughter. In any case, if we compare the delight derived from playing with the pay-off which, as we have seen before, is characteristic of work, we see that in play the pay-off amounting to delight is to some extent implied in the activity itself, while the pay-off related to work is an intended outcome of the activity, which enables us to bear the hardship inherent in the activity itself. Inasmuch as we speak of one level of playing and the concomitant delight in the movement of the body, we should be immediately aware that in this case playing is what might be described as self-reflective or at least self-referential: it activizes the organs of the body, and the delight experienced is the response of the organism to its own activity. We describe this situation as being not only self-referential but also self-reflective, since the experience of delight is not the experience of the body in the limited sense of the term but is obviously accompanied by the whole person in the psycho-physic sense, and the person, in experiencing delight, is in a way saying 'yes' to the experience. In addition, we have to be aware of another factor related to the self-activity of the organs, where a reflection or an awareness guides the activity of the organs: stretching out the hand is different from stretching the legs, because the activity is related to the potentiality of the organs. The awareness of one's potentiality is con-

4. Goffman, *op. cit.*, p. 17.

currently the awareness of one's limitations; for instance, the limit to overburdening the heart in our activity or exercise of free movement. But here, too, we have to be aware of the fact that, though playing as an exercise differs from work in that there is no end-product to the process, we cannot be oblivious of the fact that there is what is perhaps a kind of end, intended or not, of the movement, which goes by the name of 'recreation'. Re-creation is both the very process of the exercise and its outcome. Because of these two aspects of recreation it is even more difficult to posit it as the end of a process as we posit the product of work as an end.

(3)

We started by referring to the inherent relationship pertaining between playing as an exercise and the body, in order to define our conception as different from one rather influential interpretation of playing, namely that of Friedrich Schiller.[5] Let us in the first place sum up Schiller's position, following his argumentation. Man, says Schiller, is neither exclusively matter nor exclusively spirit. Beauty, therefore, being the consummation of man's humanity cannot be mere life nor can it be mere form. Beauty, according to Schiller, is the common object of two impulses, the impulse of life and that of form; therefore he introduces the term 'the play-impulse' (*Splietrieb*). This term, he goes on to say, is fully warranted by linguistic usage. In that usage the word 'play' denotes everything that is neither subjectively nor objectively contingent, and imposes neither outward nor inward necessity (*nötigt*). The contemplation of the beautiful is a happy mean between law and exigency (*Bedürfnis*). Because it is divided between the two, it is equally remote from the constraint of both. The material impulse (*Stofftrieb*) as well as the formal impulse (*Formtrieb*) are equally earnest in their demands. The former relates in its cognition to the actuality, while the latter relates to the necessity of things. In its action

5. We follow here the 15th letter of Friedrich Schiller's *On the Aesthetic Education of Man*, translated with an introduction by Reginald Snell, Frederic Ungar Publishing Company, New York, 1965, pp. 75ff.

(*Handeln*) the material impulse is directed towards the maintenance of life, while the formal impulse is directed towards the
preservation of dignity (*Würde*). Both impulses are related to
truth and perfection. But life is regarded as less important than
dignity. Duty in turn no longer compels when inclination begins
to attract. It is in this context that the aspect of beauty enters
the discourse. The beautiful, says Schiller, is neither mere life
nor shape; it is what he calls 'living shape', and he makes the
following statement concerning it: Man shall *only play* with
Beauty. And he shall play *only with Beauty*. Beauty is thus an
integrated *Gestalt* of material and form, and, as such, it evokes
the attitude and activity of play. Hence beauty — and this is an
interpretation of Schiller's position — on the objective pole as
it were, and play, as it were, on the subjective, together constitute a full expression of human possibilities as well as a full
coalescence between these possibilities and a crystallizing meaning of them. It follows therefore, to Schiller, that man plays
only when he is a man in the full sense of the word, and he is
a whole man only when he is playing.

Schiller regarded the juxtaposition of play and seriousness in
a rather dichotomic way, without paying attention to the dialectical situation inherent in the interaction between the different aspects of human activity. He says 'Man is only serious with
the agreeable, the good, the perfect; but with Beauty he plays.'[6]
Schiller exaggerated the self-enclosed character of play, and he
attempted to present play as being identical with the situation
of freedom, or to identify play with freedom, parallel to some
hints in Kant, where freedom is viewed as play. The reason for
this tendency towards the self-enclosed character of play probably lies in Kant's description of play as an occupation which is
pleasant (*angenehm*) or agreeable on its own account.[7] Or, put
differently, to regard an occupation as pleasant in itself is to
disregard the possible pay-off of the activity on the one hand,
and its encroachment on a sphere beyond itself, on the other.
Our chief interest now will be to elaborate the issue of inter-
dependence between play and everyday life and the various

6. Schiller, *op. cit.*, p. 79.
7. *Kr. der Urteilskraft*, p. 156; transl. p. 164.

aspects that accompany it as they are related to interaction between different deeds. We shall maintain that this interaction is
concomitant with an additional aspect of the evaluation of acts
and deeds, in other words, that there is no single mode of action
which, as to Schiller, is the highest manifestation of human
nature or human potentiality.

(4)

Let us start with Huizinga's comment: 'We play and know that
we play'[8] — and we may here disregard his questionable conclusion based on that statement, namely that we must be more
than mere rational beings, for play is irrational. We shall emphasize the first part of the statement: play and know that we play.
What, as a matter of fact, does that statement connote? Obviously, that we respond to the agreeable activity; our response
is an acknowledgement, therefore containing, as we have previously seen, a component of statement, assertion, recognition
of the situation — briefly, an understanding and thus a rational
or reflective act of sorts. But there is an additional aspect which
has frequently been brought forward, namely the contrast between play and fun on the one hand and seriousness on the
other. It is because of our awareness that in playing we detach
ourselves from our various interests, that we may establish an
island or peninsula of the game and adhere to what Goffman
called 'rules of irrelevance', since only dialectically in relation
to the relevant or to that which has a bearing on our ordinary
life in its 'seriousness' may we go beyond routine and establish
the rules guiding the game. They are rules of irrelevance because
of their dialectical or antithetic situation, or because rules of
relevance exist concurrently and there are relevant things which
we deliberately ignore while engaged in play. There is, therefore,
the deliberate step of establishing the structure of play which
precedes playing and constantly accompanies it. There is a de-
libarate investment of the play with certain rules that are different

8. Johan Huizinga: *Homo Ludens, A Study of the Play Element in Culture*, Paladin,
London, 1970, p. 22.

from the day-to-day performance but still contain a structural similarity to that performance. When Goffman says that games are world-building activities,[9] he is suggesting, without actually specifying, that the notion of 'world' accompanies the world-building activity characteristic of the activity of playing, since the play as such does not create the notion of world. That notion we carry within ourselves and do not erase it while engaged in playing, let alone while following the rules. In addition, the aspect of following or observing is brought in from different areas of activity and their intrinsic logic. The following of the rules of irrelevance is situated within the broad attitude of following rules. That following in turn is conditioned by our awareness of the different orbits of activity and their respective rules. It is in this sense that awareness is broader than the different fields of activity; one of the major manifestations of awareness is what might be called comparative awareness, which may be implicit or explicit. Therefore we can shift from reality to play, as well as the other way about, from play to reality, in its different shapes. It is because of the explicit position of rules in games that we speak of'war-games', and there are different activities, very significant indeed for our day-to-day existence, which because of their relation to rules we sometimes call games, using the term games as a *pars pro toto* metaphor. Here it is appropriate to enlarge the scope of our investigation and scrutinize at least several of the aspects of playing which exhibit the two-way continuity from life to games and from games to life. At this point, before going on to these additional aspects, we should reiterate one conclusion of our previous analysis, namely, that games have an impact of recreation, signifying that certain activities have repercussions on our day-to-day existence. This can be maintained in spite of the fact that we may confidently repeat the distinction between subsistence as being related to work, and fun and recreation as being related to games or play.

9. *Ibid.*, p. 27.

(5)

One rather trivial aspect of the continuity between existence and the activities embedded in it on the one hand and play on the other is the identity of the human actor who is engaged in work as well as in play; the time-gap between the two activities does not affect the identity of the actor. But let us look into an opposite aspect, which Helmut Plessner has called the anthropology of the actor (*Schauspieler*).[10] The actor embodies a person who is not himself; he plays a being or an existence other than himself by performing and, as we say, transforming himself into another person. But it is obvious that this transformation is carried by the person engaged in the performance *qua* actor. On the one hand there is a split in the actor's personality, but on the other there is the identity of the person who remains aware of himself while being aware of the role he is playing. At this point we could add that without that split the actor would cease to be an actor and become the other person, or more radically, the play would cease to be a play and become part of existence or reality. Thus in the very activity of playing — referring here to the performance of the actor — we realize that there is a transcending of the boundaries of play. Full self-enclosedness is impossible not only because of the breadth of human existence and its coordinates but also because the position or the activity of playing itself, which presupposes existence, is carried out by actors involved in it and again evolkes a resonance in or among the actors.

The aspect of identity between activities on the level of existence and the character of activity on the level of play, comes to the fore in an additional consideration. Games, and here again

10. 'Zur Anthropologie des Schauspielers', included in Helmuth Plessner: *Zwischen Philosophie und Gesellschaft, Ausgewählte Abhandlungen und Vorträge,* Francke Verlag, Bern, 1953, pp. 180ff. At this point we may add the following comment: As we emphasize the continuity from reality to play in terms of actors, we must also emphasize the continuity in the reverse direction, at least from the point of view of the theory of *catharsis*. Catharsis is meant to purify the *cathemata* or passions of the spectator who is obviously outside the scene, the performance and the team, but who is, directly or indirectly, concerned or addressed to — at least *post factum*, that is to say, after the play has been written and performed.

Goffman is correct in his analysis, give the players an opportunity to exhibit attributes valued in society in general. These attributes are, for instance, dexterity, strength, knowledge, intelligence, courage, and self-control. Since these attributes belong to the relevant segments of human reality, they obtain a kind of an official expression within the milieu of the game, which is characterized as a milieu of encounter. These attributes, as Goffman adds, may even be earned within the encounter, later to be claimed outside it.[11] Further elaborating this statement we can add that there is a continuity of human capacities brought into playing from day-to-day existence, as there is also an import in the two senses of the term, 'bringing in' and significance, of the modes of behaviour and skills exhibited in the game situation in the everyday situation. We may be engaged in a game because it is agreeable or pleasant in itself. But to make it so calls for a continuity or continuous transformation of the human capacities brought into the game. We may, as a matter of fact, take out of the game the aspect to which we referred earlier in the context of bodily existence, i.e. that of recreation, and, in a more comprehensive version, we can perhaps term it a reinforcement of capacities and skills relevant in quotidian existence. Even when we do not expect this consequence, it can still emerge, because of the impossibility of separating the game situation from the life situation and because of the interaction imposed between the different modes of activity once they are encompassed by the broad life situation.

The game, being an isolated situation, adds to the life situation a certain refinement of the skills already present in the player's former situation, precisely because the isolated encounter enables the devotion of energy and effort to aspects of style and manner. It is therefore no accident that questions of technique, in the sense analyzed before as skill and elegant performance, become prominent in different manifestations of playing, not least in playing musical instruments. Here, too, because of the rules present and the techniques developed and exhibited, we cannot say that playing is an irrational − i.e. non-structural − activity exercised just 'for pleasure'.

11. Irving Goffman: *Strategic Interaction*, Basil Blackwell, Oxford, 1970, p. 68.

(6)

It is now our task to trace different lines of extension or levels of continuity leading from day-to-day existence *qua* 'seriousness' to the activity of playing *qua* 'irrelevance'. In this context we must speak of the carry-over of certain human characterological qualities. Integrity is a case in point, being an important attribute of players. In this context it amounts to the strength of character or the propensity of the players to remain loyal to the rules or to their party, once they have agreed to do so or to play for it, or negatively, not to embark on courses of action in some other party's interest.[12] Certainly, we must distinguish between integrity proper and loyalty proper. Integrity here connotes behaviour according to rules and to a commitment. (Cheating is, of course, the opposite of integrity *qua* honesty; cheating may also be viewed as the opposite of loyalty: once we betray somebody, we behave with a lack of integrity but also with a lack of regard to our commitment to somebody outside ourselves.) Integrity is a quality of the agent in reference to himself, though it has a certain bearing upon his attitude and behaviour towards his fellow-man, while loyalty is in the first place an attitude of stability and fidelity *vis-à-vis* the partner. In any case, both integrity and loyalty are qualities of character and behaviour transposed from everyday existence to the domain of play, though perhaps their presence or absence is more visible and immediately manifest in playing, both because of the limited time-span of the activity as well as because of the deliberately defined rules to be observed. Put differently — the rules are by the same token norms of behaviour and yardsticks for the performance.

An additional aspect of the continuity of the line from day-to-day existence to play and vice versa is the whole notion, again analyzed by Goffman, of pay-off. Goffman distinguishes between intrinsic pay-off, that is to say, where the consequence of play and the gains of play are part of the situation as such, and extrinsic pay-off related to the social situation, where social

12. *Ibid.*, p. 97.

enforcement agencies may emerge, including the pay-off of money, the value of which the parties engaged in the play or game are expected to accept. We can add here that money is obviously a commodity whose meaning is outside the enclosed orbit of the game and is thus interwoven with the whole social situation, including its buit-in enforcement.[13]

Since we are engaged in the consideration of qualities or modes of behaviour, we must refer to an additional feature of the game situation which cannot be excluded from the corresponding, even basic, features encountered in the activity of work and its concomitant aspect of exchange and reward. We refer here to the interaction between the aspect of collaboration and that of contest – aspects which are obviously present in what goes by the name of party games. In contrast to the working situation and the activity of working which carries that situation, we find in the orbit of play a deliberately outlined division between the aspect of collaboration and that of contest. Neither is a *post factum* consequence, as is the encounter between agents engaged in work and its economic amplification. The division of roles is part of the rules and can thus be seen as a deliberate separation of aspects present in the day-to-day situation and transplanted by amplification and separation to the level of playing. Even more distinctly, since we have before our eyes the interaction between collaboration and contest, we regulate them by rules and expect the partners, i.e. players, to incorporate the prescribed position grounded in the structure of the activity of playing. Unlike the life situation where the roles emerge out of the activity, in the game situation the roles prescribe the activity and eventually turn the agents into instruments of the activity. This does not imply that the agents cease to be individuals endowed with qualities and become, as it were, only followers of the rules. Here again we should refer to Goffman's notion of game worthiness. He lists qualities belonging to that sort of worthiness, i.e. the intellectual capability to assess all possible courses of action and their consequences. This, of course, is a general human potentiality but in play it has to be exercised by the contesting parties. We may comment here that the assessment of possible courses of

13. *Ibid.*, pp. 114-117, 122.

action is a feature accompanying activities in general. Within the life situation the scope of courses of action and their consequences is practically infinite, and thus their assessment is difficult, presenting a continuous challenge to the agents. Since the number of participants in games are *ab initio* limited, it is more feasible to engage in such assessment. In games the isolation is not one of human qualities but is rather one in terms of scope circumscribing the nature of the activity as well as that of those engaged in it. If reference is made to the convention of setting aside all personal feelings and impulsive inclinations in sizing up a situation and following a course of action — this constraint again is not particular to the game situation but is an amplification or perhaps a focusing of life situation. The interaction between feelings and contents is a perennial dilemma of day-to-day decisions and courses of action stemming from them. We may suggest a distinction between the expressive character of action on the one hand and its end-related character on the other. Again, whenever rules are present, the expressive character is less prominent. A case in point is, for instance, praying according to a prescribed liturgy where one's own feelings are subject to the wording of the existing prayer. This is merely an analogy to emphasize the duality between expressions and codes; in game situations there is above all a tendency to play while the agent obeys rules or codes and thus excludes or suppresses his feelings and impulses.[14]

(7)

As a matter of fact, rules give meaning to the game or, by the same token, provide for its structure. It is because of this aspect that certain modes of behaviour which are guided by codes or rules are directly or indirectly akin to games or to plays. The most striking example is the formality governing different activities, like prayer, celebrations, official functions, etc. The acceptance of protocol, apparel, etc. is similar to the acceptance of the rules of the game, though by and large we here remain

14. *Ibid.*, p. 96.

within the life situation, invested with meanings which touch upon personal life but whose ceremonial character is obviously more universal than the individual life situation. Significant instances are related to turning-points in human existence, e.g. birth or death; the nature of these situations, though related to specific individuals, elicits the introduction of codes or ceremonies investing individual occasions with meanings transcending the individual experience. The situation is a life situation, its meaning from the experiential point of view is rooted in that situation. But the ceremonial or ritual aspect, by transforming the life situation into a festive one, elevates it to a level which, by virtue of meticulousness, the observation of codes, etc., adds a dimension which cannot be viewed as that of life situation proper. We are not, therefore, referring here to a translation of the life situation — in so far as it is dominated by rules or codes — to the orbit of play; we are rather suggesting a meeting between different levels of experience and activity.

A most significant aspect of the grounding of the play situation in the life situation is the presence in, and carrying-over to, games of the structure or coordinates of reality. We refer here to space and time. Games, though enclosed and guided by their own rules, take place within the broad framework of space. Sometimes a limited space is deliberately designed for the game — like the chessboard or the football ground. We encounter here a contraction of space by turning it into a framework as well as an instrument of the game, an instrument which, however, cannot change the basic structure of space as a form of simultaneity or co-existence. But the activity of locating the game in space is an activity of delineation, of keeping frontiers between the ground occupied by the game and its surroundings. The delineation is, of course, guided by the principles of the game (thus, to give a trivial example, the chessboard is smaller than the tennis court). We actually start out from the structure of the game and adjust the structure of the space to the game, obviously without being able to change the universal form of space by disregarding its character as a form of extension.

Mutatis mutandis, with some important differences, the same applies to time. Among the rules of games, there are very often rules determining the time-span of the game: 90 minutes or 40 minutes, etc. Thus, one of the rules of the game is its length in time. Time serves here as an inherent dimension of the activity of the game as such. Yet the performance of the game may sometimes call even for a discrepancy between the time it takes from start to finish measured by the clock and the immanent time of the game as such, for instance when a stoppage occurs for consultation or for the teams to exchange sides; the duration of the stoppage does not count for the prescribed time-length of the game in its totality. Thus more time elapsed by the clock than is reckoned for the game, according to its rules. Still, time as such has not been erased, neither have self-enclosed time-coordinates of the game been established. There is a difference between the actual time dimension and the fact of not counting the length of the time-span elapsed. Thus the isolation of the game becomes prominent in two features: the overriding limitation of the time-span and the disregarding of certain time lapses within the time of the game. But there always remain the extensional and structural grounding in, and relation to universal time. These features were considered in order to mitigate the usual tendency to describe play, as in Huizinga for instance, as a voluntary activity or occupation, executed within certain fixed limits of time and place, according to rules freely accepted but absolutely binding, having its aim in itself and accompanied by a feeling of tension, joy, and the consciousness that it is 'different' from 'ordinary life'.[15] We shall now go on to some remarks on this statement or description which are related to our previous comment on Huizinga's presentation.

(8)

Playing is obviously a voluntary activity. Yet we must not lose sight of, but even stress, the fact that voluntary activity as such is a very broad concept indeed. Voluntary activities take place within real time and space, or within reality — and it is immaterial

---

15. On the phenomenon of play, cf. Hans Georg Gadamer: *Truth and Method*, Continuum, New York, 1975, pp. 91ff. It is said there: 'What is merely play is not serious. Play has its own relation to what is serious'.

whether or not voluntary activity will eventually be interpreted as deterministically confined. The agent may perform a voluntary activity within the life situation, remaining within that situation and trying to give it a certain direction. The voluntary acts and habits characteristic of playing lead the agent or the agent's partners away from reality, to a withdrawal which is not introversion, but turns to a visible and open activity — remote, however, from real life. There is indeed an intrinsic connection between the act leading to the separation from everyday life of the activity of playing and what is described by Huizinga as free acceptance of absolutely binding rules. The acceptance of the rules is a voluntary act. The players or the inventors of the games set up the rules by projecting the games, but as a matter of fact the playing individual is supposed to follow the rules; he does not invent them. The invention of the rules is a kind of constitutive act and as such affords a larger extent of freedom than that enjoyed by the participants in the activity of playing, who freely accept the rules set for them. Though in this context one can ask to what extent the invention of the rules is determined by a certain logic, manifesting itself in the division of labour within teams as well as in prescribed movements. There may be some arbitrariness in the rules, for instance in chess, where the bishop has to follow certain rules, while the queen follows others. But once roles and directions are designated, this very determination calls for, or is concomitant with, a negation, since it would be futile to ascribe identical roles to different figures in the game, though the prescribed roles of those figures overlap in some areas. In any case, the freedom of invention of rules is imbued with a certain structure, while the freedom of their acceptance is a conditioned freedom in the sense that we are at liberty to decide whether or not to play the game. But once we decide to do so we are bound to follow its rules. Here we have to distinguish between the initial freedom and the ensuing subjection to the rules — according to the broad maxim *beim Ersten bist du frei.*

The next point to be analyzed is the notion of 'absolutely binding rules'. How can invented rules be absolute in the sense that they have to be unconditionally observed? Perhaps one could suggest a quasi-paradoxical explanation for the sense of obligation which pervades the activity of playing: precisely because rules are set or invented, they are absolutely binding and there are no dilemmas as to whether or not to follow them, or which of the rules have to be followed in a particular situation. In a real life situation we may find ourselves in the dilemma whether or not to follow a norm such as justice, or to exercise forgiveness because we encounter a living person implicated in a plight or predicament. We are not responsible for the existence of the person and we may respond to his existence as it is imposed on us by forbearance or understanding, which are attitudes and not exactly norms. But we may follow a norm according to the Hebrew saying: 'shall justice pierce the mountain'. Since the life situation is broad, multi-faceted, even the binding norms have to be re-interpreted, according to the particular circumstances of the case. Not so in games where the situation is invented and the actions of the partners involved are defined by the rules they have to obey; the rules are absolutely binding, and there is no question as to which circumstances they apply and *pari passu* no dilemma for an interpreter facing the binding norm on the one hand and on the other the impact of actuality, e.g. of the person evoking in him the response of forgiveness. In some games the referee is charged with ensuring that the rules are in fact obeyed, since no rules are obeyed automatically. The persons involved in the game are real persons rooted in the life world. Hence they may be motivated by factors of real life — like the urge to win, ambition etc. The absoluteness of the binding rules is therefore the thematic or obligatory correlate of the abstract or separated character of play; the two are interrelated. This is however only a partial description of playing, giving no heed to the joy, delight, etc. that accompany this activity. One of the aspects of playing is relief from the dilemmas of ordinary life, from the problematic situations of applying norms or measuring up to them under the continuous pressure or necessity of applying them concretely. As we have seen, we discern aspects of skills and techniques in the life situation, but we now realize that those do not do justice to the complexity of the concrete situation. Interpretation becomes one of that situation's major aspects, and concurrently, one of our major tasks and perplexing dilemmas in it. We face the question of interpreting for ourselves which line of action to take, or even in which profession we should play our role in the life situation. We interpret the outcome of our activity, its effects and effects of effects, etc. Thus even when we do not exhibit perplexity *vis-à-vis* interpretations, we are willy-nilly caught up in that perplexity. Once we move into the sphere of games, the perplexity of interpretation disappears and is replaced by skills and techniques which amount to the best response to the rules, in the context of the interaction between the partners. We would not enjoy playing were it not for the implicitly reflective attitude toward that activity, an attitude which has two interrelated directions: first, we know the rules and accept their dictate, and second, we know that we are moving in a sphere which differs from the sphere of norms and their application and realization in real life. The separation of the playing activity from the life situation is reinforced by the immediacy of the impact of norms in play, whereas in life situations the impact is often mediated by the situation and by our striving to find the adequate application of the norms. Huizinga is right in emphasizing the consciousness that the activity of playing is different from ordinary life. But we have to be more specific about the meaning or the 'hard core' of that consciousness and about the two-way street — to which we have already referred several times — from ordinary life to the different sphere of play and from that sphere to ordinary life. One of the foci of the consciousness of that difference relates precisely to the meaning of the freedom involved, amounting to the awareness of the difference between freedom in shaping a situation in the life state-of-affairs and freedom in constructing a semi-secregated sphere embedded in the broad contours of reality and still remaining only a 'monad' with windows *vis-à-vis* reality and within it. Let us recall in this context that Schiller criticized Kant (and Kant replied very elegantly to that criticism) by saying that Kant's morality and the centrality of the notion of duty lacked what Schiller called *Anmut*, which we may translate as grace. Schiller wanted to attribute grace to morality and thus thought that the activity of playing would *a fortiori* be imbued with grace, even more so than, he alleged, should and could be moral activity. But when we take into account the difference between the life situation and the sphere of play, we come to the conclusion that in the life situation even a sincere realization of norms is every so often accompanied by hardship, by predicaments that must be faced, and thus by what may be seen as lack elegance of performance; the playing activity is exempt from all these aspects of the realization of norms in real life, and therefore, it can be seen as imbued with *Anmut*. But in saying this we indicate the hiatus between the life situation and the activity of playing, and this has to be emphasized because in our earlier analysis we were concerned with the opposite side of the coin, namely with the continuity from the life situation to the playing activity.

(9)

Here we have to take one step further: the activity of playing, seen as a continuity from the life situation, is not an intervention in the life situation. The very construction of such an enclave is, as we have said, a deliberate withdrawal. Neither is the activity of playing, as it follows ready-made rules, a realization of moral norms, since that realization is not subject to set rules; — at this point anticipate a later discussion. Hence the activity of playing is not a consummation and amplification of the human potential as Schiller tried to present it, but is an in-between activity — between life situations and their corresponding acts and deeds, and the moral activity with all the problems that go with it. Hence we must suggest an adequate mode characteristic of playing inasmuch as the sphere of that activity is concerned. We suggest describing it as an activity related to and creating inter-subjectivity, as different from objectivity. The latter refers to given facts or pre-existent norms with all the differences pertaining between contexts of facts and imperatives of norms. The inter-subjectivity characteristic of the activity of playing is the consequence of the involvement of partners in performing acts and deeds, guided and dictated specifically and meticulously by the norms. The inter-subjective sphere springs from the willingness of the partners to engage in a shared activity which, as such, implies that the structure of that activity is prescribed by binding rules. In other words, we may say that the binding character of the rules presupposes a consensus of the partners, and the very entrance into that sphere of consensus presupposes a primary common intent to be involved in the activity at stake. The first layer of consensus is therefore the very withdrawal from reality which as such is already guided by the anticipated consensus regarding the acceptance of the rules. Here, too, there is a difference between the objective and the inter-subjective spheres. The former requires an acknowledgement while the latter refers constantly to the consensus and its structure. The interaction between partners in reality contains, to say the least, a component of voluntary individual response, while the interaction between the partners in the inter-subjective sphere is fundamentally, and perhaps exclusively, based on a prior unconditional acceptance of the interaction and of the rules prescribed for that interaction. Reality can be rejected, obstructed, resisted, etc. A consensus by definition does not admit any of these possible attitudes. Here too we have to take exception to Schiller's idealization of playing since we cannot see in play any reference to trans-personal norms when the players are totally immersed in the inter-personal orbit. Though there have been attempts at effacing the distinction between objectivity and inter-subjectivity, the analysis of the activity of playing makes us aware, by way of an example at least, that this distinction must be maintained and that it has an additional bearing upon the definition of the difference between the activity of labour and the activity of play. The former is an intervention in the objective world with its coordinates of space and time, based upon an awareness of what matters, what are the available opportunities etc. The activity of labour does not only presuppose reality, but faces it and attempts to use its openness in order to gain advantage. The activity of playing presupposes reality but against that presupposition it constructs for visible partners an activity which is guided by invisible norms. But neither the activity nor the norms are meant to change reality. The activity of playing constructs a 'monad', but does not intervene in the reality of actual situations. At most it can be said that inasmuch as the activity of playing uses materials or tools of reality, e.g. money, the results have an effect on reality. But that effect lies beyond the boundaries of the game and leads back to the life situation, at least where the pay-off (both pay and e.g. satisfaction) is not only the enjoyment immanent in the game but the addition to reality in the strict sense of the term made by the outcome of the game as a pay-off.

A few additional comments are apposite at this point, once we emphasize the inter-subjective quality of play as distinguished from objective facts and rules. It is obvious that the inter-subjective rules are binding only for those who are engaged in playing. The public, for instance, watching the play, usually knows the rules and responds to them in its acclamation or reprobation, though it is not involved in the activity subject to the rules. This is because the rules are constructed or invented carrying with themselves their sphere of application and their reference to the players. In this sense, inter-subjectivity lacks the primary common ground which is the correlation of facts of reality with prescriptive norms which call for universal action and compliance, — as is the case, for instance, with the categorical imperative. The inter-subjective sphere presupposes the presence of the agent and of the partner. Their presence as such is, as we have seen, a continuation of the reality to which the agents belonged before they became agents or partners in the game. The rules of the game precede the activity of the performance of the game, but they are binding because of our involvement in the game. Therefore, as to inter-subjective rules, they may even change — as is the case in many games undergoing some transformation in terms of, for instance, penalties, etc. In addition, we have to observe that the rules of the game create a *Gestalt* or a closed totality and they apply in their totality to the activity of playing since they prescribe the very sphere in which the activity takes place. This is not the case with reality or with moral laws. Reality is never present in our experience in its totality nor in our approach to it. Reality is, at most, the total horizon of our interventions in it but not an actual ingredient of acts of intervention. The same applies, *mutatis mutandis*, to moral norms and perhaps even more specifically so, since moral norms in their totality may be unknown, and in situations of uncertainty we sometimes have to choose one norm as binding while deliberately disregarding another. We may give medical aid to the supposed criminal without applying to our encounter the other norm of approaching him as a social or moral transgressor. The sum-total or totality of moral laws is both unknown and, as a matter of principle, unrealizable in specific acts because of their limited and limiting character. Yet both reality and the totality of moral norms, being objective in the sense introduced in the present analysis, are a potential reservoir, and thus cannot and need not be actually present in fragments of our life situations as well as in fragments of our acts of realization. The constructed scope of inter-subjective rules, as distinct from reality and from moral norms, is essentially present in its totality because the game as such is structured around the rules, though it presupposes and evokes the activity of performance.

We thus have to reiterate the constructed character of games and *pari passu* their inter-subjective nature. The two features are interrelated and lead us to our next step, in the direction of exploring the nature of politics.

CHAPTER SIX

POLITICAL ACTIVITY

(1)

We start our analysis of political activity by asking the question: in what sense can activity be attributed to politics or to the political sphere? This question becomes even more acute when we keep in mind the context of our analysis and the modes of activity we have already treated. We have seen labour and work as motivated by needs and producing, at least to some extent, products meant to satisfy these needs; together with the process of production certain techniques are evolved. We have seen that the activity of playing sometimes involves the agents in their own bodily existence, and sometimes involves them in the inter-action between their segragated sphere of activity and the norms governing that activity. The aspect of activity is, to some extent, two-fold — in the performance and in the creation of rules. Hence it is only proper to ask: what does political activity create? Does it create — at least partially — material products or inter-subjective rules? Moreover, as we have seen, structurally there is a difference between labour and play. Labour intervenes in reality, while play presupposes it and moves further towards a construction of 'monadic' spheres of games, whose whole *raison d'être* lies in that very character.

Political activity, if such there is, is a real life activity. Initial-ly it can be said that from and within the human reality — which is obviously part of the overall reality — it creates certain structures or modes of performance. Yet there is a difference between intervention in reality by work and labour and by poli-tical activity, which we are about to analyze now. Let us there-fore start with some preliminary distinctions and descriptions which may throw some light on the question.

The presupposition of the activity described as political is the fact or the reality of the existence of a multiplicity of human persons living next to each other. One can assume that the activity of work is performed even by an isolated Robinson Crusoe. But political activity presupposes the coexistence of human beings and is thus non-solitary. This coexistence is presupposed, and political activity is in the first place an intervention within the sphere or scope of that coexistence. The activity of play also presupposes the existence of other human beings and invites them to shape their coexistence according to the rules. But, as we have seen play separates its activity from real coexistence by creating a secluded sphere, lasting for a limited time. Political activity presupposes coexistence and addresses itself to it. Hence it is meant to be an intervention within coexistence and is faced with the question of the cause or end of that intervention.

In speaking of the cause, we should here recall the interesting parallel — alleged or suggested — between work and political activity. By analogy with the notion that work is initiated by needs, and these are its effective cause, at least one type of political philosophy made an attempt to isolate a human need leading to political activity and the establishment of the state. We refer here to Hobbes and the import of his analysis. Society or states are viewed as creations of men, and are thus in a sense 'an artificial animal'. Society and state are mainly understood as instruments for human survival in the elementary, that is to say, physical sense of the term, since both serve the purpose of allaying man's basic fear of violent death at the hands of his fellowmen. A primordial goal is embedded in political activity, namely, survival, and that goal motivates the creation of an artifact which is the state. In its radicalism, this is a somewhat paradoxical conception, since — at least implicitly — it presents the creation of the state as having a more basic motivation than work or labour. Both are meant to safeguard survival, but work and labour are meant to provide means for the survival of the organism, driven by continuous need due to exposure to the environment and to the fact that the organism is not self-sufficient and cannot recreate itself organically out of its own resources. The survival to which Hobbes' theory refers is a survival in the sense of overcoming not only the imagined fear of a violent death but the fear of the actual and visible threat that such a death will occur. The need for establishment of the state is to guarantee the physical presence of the *organism*, while the need underlying labour is that of the *nourishment* of the organism. But we must go a step further. The threatened human being, that is to say, another person's actual presence and actual or possible performance of certain human acts, among them, unfortunately, one that may lead to violent death. Hence the description and the instrumental analysis suggested by Hobbes presuppose the coexistence of human beings, in itself not created, while political acts and their end are channelled in such a way as to prevent violent death brought about by another human individual or individuals involved in the texture of that primary coexistence. The instrumentality of the Leviathan is constructed to promote a feeling of living together which is not perpetually threatened by humanly caused violent death.

Having referred to the pre-condition of coexistence as the point of departure for our analysis of the political activity and sphere, we must indicate the distinction between that point of departure and the Aristotelian one, which can be viewed as the opposite of Hobbes' analysis. Aristotle, as is well known, grounds the political sphere within the very essence of man, dwelling on the continuity from man's basic rationality to this social existence. Within the concept of man's rationality Aristotle included language as a mode of expression and communication and, no less important, the affinity between language and the awareness of what is just and unjust. Thus he emphasized the fact that social and political reality is the corollary of the rational principle, and that as such the political sphere is initially and essentially guided by norms of just and unjust. In the final analysis this principle deters men from following habits and natural impulses, since men as rational and political beings can be persuaded to take some course of action other than that imposed on them by habits and natural impulses.[1]

At this point the basic question emerges, which can perhaps be worded thus: whether a genesis of human coexistence, let

1. Spinoza, in spite of his indebtedness to Hobbes, stressed the element of fear of loneliness as a basic motivation for the emergence of the social and political state.

alone of the human political sphere, can be suggested. As a matter of fact, this is what Aristotle tries to do — he tries to show that there is an essential cause of the organized political sphere which lies in the essential connection pertaining between human rationality and the *polis*, or men within it. Yet if we understand human rationality basically as awareness, reflection, etc., we can say that this rationality is embedded in all human activities or, to be less general, in the two modes of activity already analyzed. Hence emphasis on rationality and even on communicativeness does not present the *differentia specifica* of the political sphere. We are still lacking a more specific explanation of the transition from human rationality to the political sphere, or of its genetic origin. Hence not only methodologically but also ontologically it is perhaps more advisable to have recourse not to the essence of man but rather to his factual existence, which, as such, is *ab initio* coexistence. The activity which is a political activity starts with the acknowledgement of that primary fact and is a continuous attempt to intervene in that coexistence by shaping it in the direction of an integration. Our first step will therefore be to describe political activity as a continuous intervention by the human beings involved in their coexistence with a view to making that coexistence stable and functional. At this point we shall roughly or broadly describe that end as integration.

A comparison with the inter-human aspect implied in the activity of work will throw additional light on the quality of the activity which is political. We have seen that the inter-human aspect comes to the fore in the activity of work through the aspect of contraction which is the corollary of supplementation. We become aware of the other person since he too is engaged in work, and we visualize the possibility and the actuality of supplementation and exchange. The presence of one's fellow-man, and obviously even more so his involvement in one's own activity, is therefore in the first place functional. Political activity starts, as it were, not from the functional position of one man with regard to another, but from their coexistence, irrespective of the reasons or causes for their co-presence. Hence coexistence is a mode of inter-human relations different from that of exchange or exchangeability; different principles and considerations must therefore apply to the respective spheres. This primary difference between the spheres will of course give rise to the question to what extent can political activity as a continuous integrative course be oblivious of the activity of exchangeability characteristic of work and labour. To put it differently: what kind of interactions and interrelations are present within the meeting between different modes of intervention in real life, and more pointedly in this case between work and labour as an activity grounded in coexistence of human beings and the focusing of it in the political sphere as a produced sphere.

(2)

Since our point of departure is the primary fact of human coexistence, we must emphasize that coexistence is obviously a vaguer state of affairs than that traditionally called by various terms such as *polis, communitas, societas*, etc. All these terms connote a certain structuring of coexistence which is perhaps closer to what has been termed (as for instance Suarez) *'hominum collectio'*. But precisely because we are not embarking on an attempt to explain the *collectio* genetically, we are faced with a first question, namely, to what extent is it at all legitimate to speak of political activity once there is a given gathering of people. This question is enlarged and amplified by an additional consideration which has to do with the discrepancy between coexistence and belonging to the human species as a whole. The broadest scope within which human coexistence occurs is the human race — mankind — as the sum-total of human individuals and as a sum-total of certain qualities pertaining to these individuals and making them human. But the difference between coexistence and belonging to and involvement in the human race lies in the fact that the latter is general, being due to the very presence of other humans, while the former, being limited in scale or delineated, is partial. The partialness of coexistence, though a primary fact for any intervention, is in itself due to acts, and these can be viewed as primary political acts, even when they are not explicitly such.

Let us look at two examples related to those primary acts — one in the sphere between man and nature, and the other within the inter-human sphere. In the sphere between man and nature the territorial aspect comes to the fore, which, in turn, amounts to the integration of space and area into the texture of human coexistence or *collectio*. Men live in space, but what turns this living into a mode of existence is their awareness of the section of space to which they relate, which is the common ground for their operations, and which they delineate *vis-à-vis* another collection of human beings who also happen to be involved in coexistence. It is essential to observe at this juncture that on this level of our analysis we cannot accept the view that the primary political attitude is that of distinction and tension between foes and friends, for the simple reason that only in terms of one coexistence is a demarcation *vis-à-vis* another coexistence meaningful, or, to put it in traditional philosophical terms, the determination of coexistence may lead to the negation of — or delineation — of a different coexistence pertaining to other human beings. However, the incorporation of space into the orbit of coexistence is a human deed, accomplished by individuals, and, at the same time, by inter-related individuals regarding the space of broad reality as significant for their coexistence. The primary fact is coexistence; but coexistence, when analyzed, leads to a discernment of natural components — space, soil, ground, territory, etc. — and the impact of these components upon coexistence is a linkage between human beings and nature as well as a continuous creation of a context in which that coexistence is present but which in turn is a condition for such coexistence. The activity in its nuclear form and content is the affirmation of coexistence and concurrently the integration of components stabilizing coexistence and making it possible or, to some extent, tangible — precisely because of its relation to space.

A second aspect of the activity enabling coexistence and maintaining it is the common language between human beings, which again is a partial language, as is any 'natural' language. The use of a natural language enables communication between those involved in the context of primary inter-human relations described here as coexistence. In turn it reinforces that coexistence by creating channels of communication between human individuals possessing a common language. Furthermore it delineates one coexistent context from another such context by the fact that those implicated in it use a different partial language. Language is, of course, a very much more abstract ingredient than space. Hence we refer to space as a means of integration and to language as a means of communication. Yet both aspects are primary components of human coexistence — the first being a continuous attempt to bring external reality into the human orbit while the second is *ab initio* part of the human orbit. At this point we can attempt to explain the meaning of political activity in its initial sense. Maintaining coexistence by integrating it in space and by communication is a continuous activity, or, put it the other way around, maintaining an input of space within the human context as well as the unceasing contact of communication carried out through the linguistic medium — is a continuous activity. Moreover, we can say that this level of political activity opens up vistas for additional levels which are intended to safequard the initial texture of coexistence. Here we can follow the point made by Helmuth Plessner, namely, that that which is politically relevant is that which is both significant for politics as well as which is determinable by it.[2] The basic stratum of political activity is relevant for the additional levels of that activity. Looking, as it were, from top to bottom, initial coexistence is important because it is already assessed from the point of view of those aspects which are to be determined by the process of political acts and deeds.

(3)

An additional element of the incorporation of given natural data into the context of inter-human relations is the aspect of kinship in the biological sense. This aspect is evident in the term we use, viz. lineage, which can be understood as contracting the scope of descent of human beings to a line of succession. This very shift from belonging to the human race to having a common lineage points to the fact that the human context carries within itself an aspect of partialness. Human beings consider themselves as

2. In the previously mentioned book: *Zwischen Philosophie und Gesellschaft, Ausgewählte Abhandlungen und Vorträge.*

next of kin by way of a sort of appropriation or sense of belonging which, as Claude Lévi-Strauss pointed out, is in itself an aspect of inter-human communication. But the aspect of biological descent represented by lineage is of an even more interpretative character than the introduction or integration of the dimension of space into the inter-human context. Space is the environment encircling human beings. It does not 'run in their blood' as any genetic aspect of inter-human relations is bound to do by definition. To regard the genetic descent as a component of belonging is obviously of an interpretative character, whatever the reasons or causes for that interpretation may be; for instance, the interpretation suggested by Lévi-Strauss, namely, the exchange between families, which, as such, posits a boundary between one human context *vis-à-vis* other human contexts. The women of the group circulate between clans: lineages or families are, as is well known, according to the structuralist description, analogous to the words of a group which are circulated between individuals. Again, the incest taboo implies a line of demarcation between different human contexts, which means that the truly elementary human units are not isolated families, let alone separate human individuals, but relations between them.[3] But if this is so, then kinship is even more related to awareness than language is, precisely because kinship is already an inter-personal structure which, as such, is not to be perceived by the senses, but has to be conceived as grounded in the factor of descent, which is interpreted as delineating boundaries between groups and the individuals it embraces. The aspect of the group as an abstract entity is even more evident on the level of kinship than on the level of language. Language can be activated by concrete individuals, while kinship is made prominent and gains its impact only through the prism of interpretation which contains the given aspect of common descent, the boundary which follows that element, and the norms and prohibitions grounded in it. The paradoxical situation of the biological mode of human coexistence lies, therefore, in the fact

3. Claude Lévi-Strauss: *The Scope of Anthropology*, translated by Sherry Ortherand and Robert A. Pane, Jonathan Cape, London, 1967, pp. 61, 83, 51, 41. Cf. the present author's 'On Lévi-Strauss' Concept of Structure', in *The Review of Metaphysics*, Vol. XXV, No. 3, 1972, pp. 489-526.

that it is not less tangible than the coordinates of space, but its tangibility does not make it effectice unless it passes through the prism of interpretation in terms of, and for the sake of, co-existence. This brings both factual distinctions and normative imperatives into the scope of coexistence.

Looking again at the three aspects of the given infrastructure of coexistence, we may say that political activity can be understood as being present in the interpretation referring to the dimension of reality *qua* space and to the dimension of descent *qua* lineage, if we understand political activity in the broad sense as establishing the very sphere of coexistence. To be sure, these interpretations take advantage of the linguistic medium for the sake of interpretation, and they again refer to the medium of communication as one of the components of primary coexistence. But it is perhaps impossible to attribute the sense of interpretation to political activity, and by the same token to look at it as having a creative impact, or as creating the very existence of the context. If we confine the primary activity to interpretation, we point out the reference of that activity to natural data on the one hand and the ongoing integration of those data on the other. If this is so, then continuous political activity is either an attempt to elevate the given data and the components of its contents to a higher level, for instance, by disregarding the aspect of kinship and replacing it by the aspect of citizenship, or by the activity of adding new components to the existing ones, for instance by building upon the infrastructure of kinship the super-structure of statehood, or by maintaining the different components and creating and recreating structures which will maintain them in changing modes of equilibrium. Here again we may say that the point of departure for the analysis of political activity contains a projection of the directions of that activity, if we look at it from the angle of the present or of history rather than from the angle of our point of departure.

(4)

The question that arises at this point is: who are the political agents, if any? Without indulging in what can be described as democratic idealization, we must come to the conclusion that on the level of primary coexistence and of continuous reference to its real (space) and created (language) components, no single agent or separate group of agents can be identified. The very meaning of the relationship to space and of the involvement in the linguistic medium renders the accomplishment of the deeds diffuse, that is to say, that no distinct and distinguishable agents can be held accountable for the maintenance of the creation of this fundamental stratum of political activity. The aspect of identifiable agents comes into prominence on additional levels of political activity. *Pari passu* we recognize both the problem of political activity and its inherent norm. This activity takes place among human individuals who through it create a *collectio*. The *collectio* as such does not swallow up the individuals, though they are involved in the very structure of the sphere through these two factors or modes of interaction, viz. space and communication. Within the context of coexistence, individuals are maintained or they preserve themselves, while the *collectio* is initiated or maintained. Thus the basic structure of the political sphere presents from the point of view that sphere and the various activities related to it the perpetual problem of the duality and balance between maintaining individuals and concurrently maintaining the *collectio*. No automatic equilibrium can be guaranteed; individuals are given and present, while a *collectio* is an abstract entity; thus an ontological disequilibrium is inherent in the sphere. This disequilibrium may sometimes create, as alas we very well know from history, a political overzealousness — that is to say, an attempt to safeguard the *collectio* because it is not, like the individuals, grounded in a bodily reality. Concurrently there exists the danger of an individualistic fallacy, that is, of an attempt to impose on the *collectio* the task and function of maintaining the individuals, even to the point of giving up the *collectio*, and thus eventually to abolish the *collectio*, for the shaky equilibrium can only be stabilized through continuous endeavours to maintain it. At this point the following can only be a preliminary, but nevertheless adequate, statement: Within the sphere of inter-human coexistence we move in the direction of maintaining that coexistence. An imposition of the exclusive norm of *collectio* may destroy individuals, while the imposition of the exclusive norm of maintaining individuals only may destroy the *collectio*. Having said this, we can already recognize the interaction between political activity and its inherent norm.

(5)

Before coming to topics like might, obedience, etc., some further comments are called for. In the first place, we must return to the aspect of partialness to which we have already referred, due to the presence of space on the one hand and the essential significance of language on the other. It can be said that since political activity, unlike play, is an intervention in reality which in this particular context amounts to the integration of space and the activization of the linguistic medium, partialness is essential, since we experience reality only as fragments, though we attempt to enlarge the scope of this experience and to merge the extension of our experience with the extension of reality. We do not experience the human race as a totality, but we do experience our interaction with other human beings, and in our case the interaction takes place within the delineated inter-human context. Possibly because of that tension between the partialness of experience and the real ultimate horizon, up to the present at least, no political entity which coincides with the totality of the human race has existed. It is well known that aiming at that totality has been interpreted by many adherents of the idea of progress, including Condorcet and Kant, as the norm and focus of human or historical progress. It could be said that one direction of political activity is to put different interacting human groups to use, by turning them into individual agents in the cause of exchangeability and supplementation — the rhythm which we observed within the scope of work, competition and collaboration and their economic implications. One direction of political activity can by discerned, therefore, in the application of extra-political standards to political groupings. This is significant for the interaction between and within the groups, as we shall see presently.

A second point to be observed is that the bases of cohesion of the groups, though rooted in a primary texture, are subject to historical processes and changes. The political activity itself, for instance, the establishment of sovereignty, can become a connecting factor, as we know from Max Weber's analysis of America: there, according to his findings, statehood (nation) created the people. In another area, political sovereignty and governments entrusted with sovereignty are established to overcome primary tribal differences and even clashes. Political activity, therefore, can be guided by historically determined factors meant to create, or to reinforce, the *collectio*.

It can be said that the dynamics of political activity as well as its immanent norm are related to the ongoing process of turning the *collectio* of people living in the primary coexistence into an integrated whole. Let us take as an example the fact that people not only coexist statically somewhere in space without communicating as agents involved in a sort of game, but that they establish relations within the given context of coexistence. One facet of these relations is mutual concern, which, in turn, is part and parcel of what goes traditionally by the name of *oikos* and economy. The fact that mutual concern again can be related or relevant to the assitance provided by supplementation and exchangeability is only an articulation of the fact that there are relations emerging within the network of coexistence which can be viewed either as prolongations or reinforcements coexistence. In any case, the political sphere as a continuous process towards integration incorporates different aspects of human activity, which have their own structure and logic but which become or can be made into instruments or precursors of political integration. Obviously, the aspect of mutual care is not limited to economic care or to care for subsistence in the material sense of the term and can expand to contain different aspects of care, like upbringing, education, prepration for the future, health etc. All these activities have a structure of their own. But in the context of coexistence they have an impact on, and give momentum to, the process of coexistence.

Coexistence, therefore, becomes both the point of departure and the continuous task of the political sphere, since human activities of different sorts take place within the context. Thus they bring into politics the dynamics of a historical process, both in terms of time and in terms of the changes occurring in history. Those changes, while taking place within the political context, emerge from it and in turn shape it. E. Jordan observes that politics has no particular content, or no content exclusively its own. There is no specialized type of action or form of life or kind of object that is purely political. It follows from this that any type of action or form of life becomes a political phenomenon only by virtue of its relation or possibilities of relation to the whole.[4] But precisely that relation to the whole or, as we put it before, the relationship to the context of coexistence and the continuous integration which is part of that context as well as subservient to it — is the political content proper. We cannot expect that the direction of the activity related to this context would be as specialized as the direction of work or play, since, to some extent, the political activity emerges here as a secondary activity which, on the one hand absorbs the primary activities, and, on the other, places them in a setting, or let us say order, this being of a second order in the meta-sense or in the mathematical sense. Interestingly, language in its hidden wisdom uses the term politics in the derogatory sense when 'politics' connotes a limted activity of intriguing, a sectional activity, or one related to factions or fractions of existence, that is, an activity not related to the aspect of integration. Thus the balance, shaky as it is, characteristic of the political sphere and the activity whose intentionality is that sphere, is one of maintaining different activities which have their own content, but which, at least as a matter of fact, take place within the inter-human context as components of political integration while simultaneously furthering that integration.

If this is so, then we here encounter both the wholeness of the political sphere or structure and its built-in limitations. The political sphere does not, as such, create out of its own resources

4. E. Jordan: *The Good Life*, University of Chicago Press, Chicago, 1949, p. 339.

the activities of labour or education, etc. — those activities which we subsumed before under the heading of care or concern. The political activity presupposes the primary context and the activities occurring within it. It cannot autonomously decide either to establish the context, or not to follow the rhythm of occurrences present in it. Political activity can introduce a new perspective into the context by making it explicit, for instance, by incorporating it in a state as a political entity, or by providing facilities for work, or, in modern society, establishing agencies guaranteeing work and subsistence, that is, the product of work. There is a limit to the decisiveness of the political activity precisely because it presupposes the vague structure of coexistence and the more articulate structure of activities; it is a deliberate activity. It does not establish a peninsula outside the given reality (*qua* games) but one that refers to the given reality and endows it with a direction towards integration, intervening in the given reality from, as well as for the sake of, the locus of integration. Political activity, in this sense, by introducing only perspectives, makes things, as we have seen before, determined for and determinable by, politics.

(6)

Here we face the problem of the dynamic character of the political sphere, which amounts to continuous political activity. How can this ongoing character of political activity be explained? When we speak of work as an ongoing activity, we can discern the effective and final cause of work, namely, the need which keeps re-emerging, as well as the end *qua* satisfaction or gratification, which is bottomless and demands re-production, in the literal sense of the term. Where can we place the effective and the final causes of the political sphere and its activity? This question is even more acute since, as we have seen, we start with primary coexistence; we might be led to assume that coexistence, being given, is also safeguarded and thus does not call for the reproduction and the continuous activity which supposedly serve it.

Yet the situation is not so, and without attempting to present a full explanation of the continous character of political activity in its various facets and components, we shall attempt to throw some light on causes and reasons that are pertinent to the issue. In the first place, we must refer again to our point of departure, namely, the integrative character of coexistence and the activity pertinent to it and, more specifically, to converting space as an environment, and descent as belonging, into solidifying factors of coexistence. We have seen that integration is grounded in interpretation, and only when we interpret our relation to space as well as to our kinship and descent, do the interpretated data become factors to which we refer in providing a basis for, as well as explaining, coexistence. Yet, as a matter of fact, the activity of interpretation and integration never comes to an end. If we do not visualize space as having a bearing upon our situation and our diverse activities, space becomes neutral or opaque, or perhaps we move to another space when the previous one ceases to be the hard core of our environment. The same applies to the aspect of descent, and perhaps even more markedly so. Descent may become less relevant in our awareness because of regroupings, intermarriages, or perhaps because factors of an altogether different character overshadow the significance of common descent and the aspects of coexistence based on it. For instance, religious division may be more important than common descent, and even linguistic barriers can be viewed as outweighing the common grounding in the common descent. Thus the ongoing quality of political activity refers in this context either to the continuous integration and interpretation of the primary factors, or to a repression of these factors, their obliteration, and eventually to various attempts at replacing the primary factors with factors of a different character which, in the course of history, become unifying or integrating factors.

Amplifying this point, we can say that political activity is grounded in the basic fact that primary coexistence is never totally secure or fully established. That activity is either intended to secure coexistence or to find factors that will assist in making it secure. After all, political coexistence is not a natural phenomenon in the sense that it takes care of its own reproduction or is subsumed under laws governing its behaviour. At this point primary coexistence is supplemented by intention, which here means a deliberate attempt to create foci of coexistence and, in a sense, the anticipation of that which is the expected outcome of acts and deeds guided by that intention. This is expressed by the German *Vorsatz*, which means that through our intentionality we anticipate what will or should be established or created. This continuous activity is therefore the corollary of the interpretative character of political activity, since this activity has no grounding in natural needs and cannot be teleologically directed towards products at the end of a line of production. The interpretative character of politics becomes even more significant and, let us say, tangible, than the character of the activity of work. In addition to looking for factors promoting coexistence or — to use a stronger term — cohesion, politicial activity is constantly concerned with turning the various factors, as we have already remarked, into factors of political cohesion having a logic of their own. This applies not only to inter-human relations and connections, but also to individual works and achievements; for instance, a great literary work or a scientific theory are interpreted as related to the background of the society and its cultural milieu. They are turned into symbols at least of coexistence and cohesion, they are meant to evoke a sense of belonging to a group, or a sense of integration. But *pari passu* we encounter here the opposite aspect of political activity: since, unlike Diogenes, it does not search for wisdom but for integration, it may cause divisions of opinion and even disputes over what are the factors of integration and what is the best use to be made of the existing factors. Examples of political controversies emerging from the essence of political activity are abundant. To mention again instances already suggested: the replacement of language by citizenship, or the importance attributed to religious affiliation over the linguistic community and perhaps even over genealogical lineage. From another angle: to what extent can political integration rely on a *laissez-faire* of the exchangeability of work activities and the goods produced by them, or must politics, as such, intervene in work activities and regulate them in order not to cause a clash, to say the least, between the inter-human aspect of work and the products it creates, and the aspect of integration or wholeness characteristic of the political sphere? It can be said that the more activities are contained within the political sphere the more needs emerge in the direction of integration and the more does the political activity become dominant and grounded in its own norm. This process can be described as a continuous turning of primary coexistence into a created cohesion. This is where we find the cause and the reason for the politization of human life in modern times, which is due not to the prevalence of the political over other activities, but rather to the complexity of factual connections and their effects in the sphere of inter-human relations. Hence the primary intervention has to be continuously maintained as a deliberate intervention, despite all the clashes that accompany this process, where the partial logic of separate activities may be supplanted by the integrating logic of the political sphere. We recognize this clash, for instance, in the problem of the equilibrium between work done individually and services rendered by public or government agencies. In this context a person does not have to rely — only — on his own work to satisfy his needs, since the public agencies take care of this independently of the process of needs prompting work and aimed at their satisfaction. Obviously, in addition to the aspect of integration which becomes important in the function of the providing agency, we also observe the emergence of the aspect of responsibility, which ceases to be merely related to individuals and is transposed to the public as the integrated and integrative sphere. The addition of a moral consideration to the logic of the political sphere and structure complicates the situation even more, as is usually the case with situations in which different considerations and components become pertinent.

The ongoing character of the political activity can also be explained from a different angle: even on the elementary level of primary coexistence the aspect of approval or acceptance is essential for the very presence of the sphere of coexistence. This is based on the three factors mentioned — space, language and descent. The structure of the political activity and sphere can be characterized as a process obtaining the implicit or tacit approval of the people concerned and making it manifest or, having obtained their acceptance of coexistence, making them demand to participate in its shaping. That demand can be viewed as an explication of the implicit approval and consent, but it can also be regarded as replacing them in part of completely. Participation is related to the given factors of coexistence, once we become aware of them and want to be involved in maintaining and cultivating them deliberately. It becomes a demand of an organizational character, once we want to have a share in the agencies created by, or for the sake of, the group. Here again we have to be aware of the fact that we are perhaps imposing an inherent democratic nuance on the phenomenological interpretation of the political sphere and activity. But, at least up to this point, we are bound to maintain the diffuse character of the political sphere and activity which can be interpreted only retrospectively as having a democratic character. This is so since our point of departure lies in the co-presence and co-activity of individuals within the framework of coexistence, while, objectively, we are unable to isolate certain individuals from that framework and to attribute to them a special position or impact on its reality and presence. This starting point does not by any means preclude, at least theoretically, the possibility of recognizing the hierarchical structure of coexistence. But that structure pertains to the organization of coexistence and not to its primary factual presence. And indeed, as we shall see presently, this is one of the features and problems of political activity and the sphere in which it takes place and to which it refers.

(7)

For the sake of rounding off the picture in terms of philosophical interpretation it is apposite to suggest a difference between the view presented in the foregoing analysis and the view whose main representatives are Hegel and Marx, who followed in Hegel's footsteps. We refer here to the dialectical process of turning that which is given in itself (*an sich*) into that which becomes for itself (*für sich*). The previous exposition may sound like a variant on the Hegelian theme, since as an essential aspect of the political sphere and its concomitant activity we posited the factor of intention, interpreted as *Vorsatz* (a term used by Hegel in his 'Philosophie des Rechts') and as a continuous shift from the passive presence to the integration aimed at. Yet the difference between the view suggested here and that which is a guiding theme in Hegel's philosophy has to be emphasized. In the first place, we are not referring here to a world spirit (*Weltgeist*) whose immanent dynamics leads to self-awareness. We are referring to the fact that the political sphere proper, as a specific orbit of inter-personal human activity, is imbued with an implicit interpretation. That interpretation becomes explicit because of the needs of the sphere and not because of the imperative of cognitivity or rationality, which in Hegel's view is an overriding imperative and thus holds good for all spheres, including the political. We began our analysis with the interrelation between needs and their satisfaction but we find that there is no parallel for that interrelation in the political sphere; in that sphere we discern only interactions. These, in turn, are accompanied by consciousness, because otherwise they may cease to exist and operate. In a sense it can be said that the precarious character of political existence — as being primarily an intervention in human reality and not an intervention in nature — lies in continuous need of support by all the factors that can be mobilized, including deliberation, intention, aiming at integration, as well as struggles and controversies which may be the negative results of those deliberate acts. Here we must distinguish between the instrumental importance of awareness and the intrinsic position of rationality as an aim or end of the ongoing process of human endeavour. The end of the process relevant for political activity is not rationality but integration and the difference between the two cannot be disregarded.

In addition, we can even point out a clash between the ongoing activity imbued with awareness and its impact on integration in the societal and political sense. One may wonder whether it is quite so certain that the political sphere always benefits from growing political intention and intentionality: as already suggested, the more intention there is the more controversies are bound to arise. Optimistically one can say that controversies take place 'within the family' only, and that where mutual ignorance and disregard prevail there are no controversies. But from historical experience we know very well that some controversies expand until they cause dissolution instead of cohesion. Thus the ongoing intention and awareness may, from the point of view of political integration, become self-defeating. Hence we have to make distinctions under two interrelated heads: (a) the distinction between awareness and intention and reason and rationality, and (b) the distinction between growing intention and awareness due to the problematic situation of the political sphere on the one hand, and, on the other, the evocation of intention for the sake of the political sphere and the pragmatic results of that process, which cannot be viewed as inherently safeguarding the sphere whose problems it was evoked to solve. The dialectic between the intention of the intention and its pragmatic results flies in the face of optimistic over-interpretation of the cognitive process. At this point we can move to the analysis of might and dominance as ordering factors within the coexistence of human beings.

(8)

Again, we will not attempt a genetic presentation of the emergence and existence of dominance within the social contact, that dominance which, as a matter of fact, turns social coexistence into a political entity proper. It is clear that since we started with the facticity of coexistence, we started from a line which can be called horizontal, seeing human beings in their dispersed and diffuse interaction. The element of governing brings a vertical component into prominence within the inter-human context, one related to hierarchy, since governing implies a sort of imposition of decisions or orders upon people who, at least as a matter of principle, are free to reject those orders or decisions. In thise sense governing structures coexistence, intervenes in it, and does not rely on the processes of mutual adjustment which are usually present in the context of coexistence. Since dominance in its essence is an ability or potentiality to dispose and can become an actuality of disposing, we realize that the position of dominance, though referring to coexistence, confronts coexistence. Thus it is a factor that cannot simply be viewed as being integral to coexistence or to cohesion.

Since we do not attempt — and would not such an attempt be futile? — to explain the emergence of might and rule, we follow the logic implied in the theory of the social contract.

Obviously we do not refer to the fact of the occurrence of the social contract nor, correspondingly, to the fact of the occurrence of dominance; we refer to those aspects of coexistence which can bring about the factual presence of dominance in the political sphere. Let us start, therefore, with one of the factors we referred to before, namely, the biological or genealogical lineage. Unlike space, which is the coordinate of the environing reality and calls for continuing integration in the inter-human context, the biological factor does not evoke integration but — if at all — an awareness of dependence. Another aspect of this factor is the awareness that those present here and now did not create themselves and are implicated in a line which, at least to some extent, contains an element of dependence. Lack of total sovereignty is therefore an aspect of genealogical dependence and may, at least potentially, lead to the additional or enhanced awareness that we do not have sole authority over our own existence, once we understand also the etymological root of the term 'authority' (author = originator) which amounts to *Urheberschaft*. We are not trying to say that dependence and the awareness of it are identical with authority and the aspect of ordering grounded in it, and as such give rise to respect for or acceptance of the orders given. What we intend to say is that the separation of the hierarchical aspect of dominance from the inter-human context is not a totally new beginning, lacking an initial foundation in the primary datum of coexistence. Moreover, the very possibility of distinguishing between genealogically rooted dependence and the authority commanding respect already occurs on the primary level of inter-generational connections, prior to the organized level of dominance in a political entity. The more creation and deliberate expression are involved, the more questionable the authority becomes, since, being created, it has to justify itself continuously. Goethe says somewhere that only a pedantic person demands an authority everywhere.[5] But we can say that because of the increasing impact of deliberations as well as of intentional acts within the political sphere, the demand for legitimized power, pedantic as it may sound, is indeed a continuing demand. Even when we do not question the authority of the

---

5. 'Maximen und Reflexionen', *Werke Bd. XII*, Verlag C.H. Beck, 1981, p. 415.

locus of power, we may question the legitimacy of the particular or individual manifestations of that power in the form of orders given here and there. This argument can be differently expressed: even when we grant the very institution of government as embodying the hierarchical principle in the political context, we may question the authority of the governor or at least demand an exposition of the legitimacy, i.e. authority, both of his position and of its individual manifestations.

To the extent that we refer to the line of continuity — continuity taken very broadly — from the awareness of dependence on biological origins to the awareness of dependence on the ordering power, we may say that political organization and along with it political activity appear as following a line which can be described as one of articulation. The political sphere, being tied up with intentions, articulates the aspect of dependence, shifting it from its inert presence in the very structure of human coexistence, and turning it into a focused entity related to coexistence, growing out of it, but still facing it — not to say separated from it. Ontologically speaking, we encounter here a basic issue, namely, whether or not we should see the presence of power in the political sphere as an expression of the ontological position of the individual, as for instance Helmuth Plessner suggested, or rather as a continuation of the different aspects involved in coexistence and therefore as a continuation of that coexistence and not as an expression of the anthropology or anthropological character of man. Plessner thought that since every human being is a power (*der Mensch als Macht*), that basic character of man appears, and is even bound to appear, within the political sphere. Obviously might is to be understood in this context as a capacity or potentiality written large, and thus as a continuation of a basic feature of the human essence. Yet we cannot follow this line, because our point of departure does not lie in the position of the individual and his self-awareness, but in inter-human relations. Whatever is present within the political sphere must be grounded immanently within that sphere and must not lead us to transcend that sphere in order to find a root within the essence of man, if that essence can at all be a guiding point of departure in our analysis.

But the line of articulation has to be supplemented by what

we here suggest the line of functionality. Human beings implicated in the inter-human context are aware that this context, primary as it may be, does not organize itself automatically or, put differently, does not appear to be identical with an order proper, that would define the positions to be occupied by various individuals in the interest of the preservation of coexistence to such an degree that concurrence and cohesion would be more dominant than clashes, competition, let alone dissolution. The establishment of a locus of power is therefore functionally related to an attempt at turning coexistence into an order — and let us not forget that one of the original meanings of order is to issue commands. The awareness of the interrelation between cohesion and subjection is one of the critical points in the structure of the political sphere and the activity serving it. That interrelation amounts in practice to a tacit or explicit preference given to order for the sake of cohesion over the factual coexistence which lacks order and may undermine cohesion. Underlying the existence of political order and whatever goes with it is a kind of pessimistic defiance of the *laissez-faire* attitude, grounded in the realization that coexistence, factual as it may be, does not take care of itself, and that its maintenance and preservation depend on continuous intervention. Power becomes an instrument regulating the perseverance of coexistence. As such, it changes the very essence of coexistence by organizing it and by intervening in its organization for its own sake. At this point let us revert for a moment to Hobbes' emphasis on the fear of violent death, by attempting to interpret it somewhat more broadly. The presence of the inter-human context certainly does not eliminate the possibility of violent death. The establishment of a social and political organization does not in itself guarantee protection from violent death. It is an attempt to create a functional preserve which may, by its very presence, prevent the incidence of violent death or generally of acts which undermine coexistence. Power here becomes in one sense a preemptive instrument, and in another an intervening instrument. But both these aspects, related to the presence of power, are of a functional character since they are meant to be subservient to the process starting from coexistence and leading to cohesion — a process which has neither beginning nor end.

Here again, the involvement of political structures and activities in history becomes apparent. The factors undermining coexistence are continuously present for the simple reason that individuals do not disappear within coexistence — they are interwoven in relations but they remain the foci of those interrelations. Hence they may take exception to the various modes of coexistence to the various modes of coexistence or may prefer one mode over another. In addition, there is the ever-present possibility of questioning the legitimacy of the intervention of power in the social context and thus of exposing power to what we call social forces operating within the horizontal order, but also facing the vertical one. A softer interpretation of the instrumental position of power can be to view it, therefore, as directed towards the channeling of clashing persons and interests into the given coexistence. A stronger interpretation of that instrumentality may be to view it as an attempt at creating common channels meant not only to prevent clashes but also to reinforce the initial coexistence on its never-ending way to cohesion. Just the same both interpretations of the instrumentality of power have a common denominator, namely, that the justification for the exercise of power is a general lack of confidence in the ability of human spontaneity to bring about an agreement preserving coexistence and shaping it according to mutual agreement. The paradoxical character of political activity is grounded mainly in the instrumentality of power: political activity attempts to establish consent to put an end to the ongoing process of consenting or being engaged in continuous argument and to make room for decisions that will cut the Gordian knot of argument. Hence it is presupposed that there should be agreement or consent to subjection to power; and that there should be different devices to prevent the possibility of a separation of the power from the context, such as rotations, constitutional divisions, etc. Within that framework, however detailed it may be, the consent to end the argument and not to rely on spontaneity alone, concurrently accepting orders willingly, represents the dialectical inner structure of the political sphere.

It goes without saying that the functional or instrumental aspect of government is prominent in what we call international relations, which in many cases are conducted by governmental bodies with a view of achieving certain goals or, in a broader sense, for the sake of the very nexus between political entities. Naturally, the military domain and all that it implies, are part of the functional context of the political sphere and its activities. Here we are already touching on an additional aspect of governing, which can be described as manifestation or emanation. Governments, in a sense, make explicit the context and cohesion of human coexistence. They function on the one hand by turning it into a political entity and on the other by representing the entity. They symbolize the entity *vis-à-vis* those who dwell within it and *vis-à-vis* those outside it. Empirically speaking an entity is always delineated. It occupies a certain space, and in its delineation it faces nature or another entity. This general comment on the position of entities pertains also to political entities in spite of the obvious difference between a personal entity, carrying in and with itself its own body, and a political entity which lacks a body, though we use the term 'body' as 'body politic' or as a synonym for an agency. The political entity, abstract as it is, attempts as it were to overcome its abstractness through its various functions and techniques by introducing more and more concrete actions, without ever being able — and aiming — to eradicate its inherent basic abstractness. It creates governments as one more attempt to make its position concrete by establishing an institution which in its manifestation and emanation contracts the diffuse entity and makes it an agent — and a government is an agent.

One of the manifestations of the basic character of government as an emanation and expression is the aspect of ownership which to some extent pertains to governments, though that aspect has to be taken with a grain of salt. Its most salient expression is the relationship between the political entity and the government expressing and representing it on the one hand and the territorial basis of the entity on the other. In a way, the territorial basis or the territorial extension of that basis into the sea and ocean entail in themselves a component of ownership, at least *vis-à-vis* other political entities which cannot, or are not allowed to, encroach on the territorial basis and the territorial waters. This is not exactly analogous to ownership in the private sphere where commodities can be sold, though sometimes parts of the territorial basis can be sold to private owners or, at least, be placed at their disposal. But to sell the territorial basis in its entirety would amount to giving up the political entity altogether — and here we find the limitation in the concept of ownership as it pertains to the political entity. But with all due reservations, in that entity there is at least one component whose position is clearly analogous to that of the owner in the private sphere: the very evolution of government establishes its right to dispose — in the positive and the negative sense of the term. Obviously, the functional aspect of issuing orders goes along with the expressive aspect of that activity, since issuing orders as such is a manifestation of that entity.

In a broader sense, the expressive aspect of government amounts to what is called sovereignty, the latter being both the very expression of the existence of the political entity as well as the right to activize that entity in two directions: towards the constituents of the political entity as well as towards other political entities. At this juncture we must return to the functional aspect of governing and suggest the following parallelism between functions and expressions. Functions serve an objective or an end, such as, in the very broad sense, the very existence of the political entity or in a more limited sense, protection, welfare, etc. Once this correlation exists between functions and their objectives, the agencies and anonymous human beings carrying out the political activity introduce into its sphere the component of techniques; these amount to instrumental skills and can be conceived as integral parts of modes of behaviour whose justification lies in the ends they serve. As against this, governments as expressions are characterized by rules rather than by techniques and functions, though it is clear that a sharp line can hardly be drawn between these two aspects. Rules are constitutions, precedents, and all those aspects which represent the code of the political entity and which prescribe the position of the government, since without rules a government would only be a person or a group of persons lacking in this sense the expressive character of government. In addition, as ends justify instruments and are part of the authority of government, rules justify the representation or make the government representative, thus underscoring the expressive component inherent in government. Again, both the functional and the representative aspects of government are implicated in a characteristic tension which is due to the insurmountable abstractness of political entities and of the activities they aim at. The carriers of both the instrumental activities and of the expressive position and its emanations are individual human beings. The reference to the ends to be served is a continuous attempt to understate the role of the individual human beings by turning them into agents within agencies, subservient to the end. The functional aspect of government transforms individual human beings into functionaries, without, of course, necessarily assuming a total identity between the ontological framework of the political sphere. Depersonalization, if this term may be permitted, already occurs on the level of government in its instrumental capacity; the political activity, along with those engaged in it, bestows their consent — explicit or not — on that logic of instrumentality. The same structure applies, with all due differences, to the expressive character of government. The rules, the legal system, and the agencies serving it, are obviously embodiments of trans-personal norms, to which the government, the legislature, or the courts of law are meant to be subservient. But here again the impersonal character of the rules is activized and interpreted by concrete i.e. individual human beings. Participation in activization and interpretation becomes a political objective and a focus for the political struggle, even when all the rules are taken for granted and those engaged in the various activities take it upon themselves to observe them, both in their pronouncements and in their behaviour. There is no escaping this continuous shift towards concrete human beings, because the depersonalized political sphere as such cannot take care of itself except through the mediation of individuals as concrete human beings. Depersonalization is the correlate of the abstractness of the political entity which carries weight by prescribing behaviour in terms of ends and rules. Yet it succumbs to the concreteness embodied in the concrete human beings who in turn are the carriers of activity even when they are not identifiable with the end and with the rules.

A difference between the instrumental and the expressive aspect of government must again be mentioned at this point. Functions are by definition activities and so are techniques.

They are exercised to serve ends and are essentially of a dynamic character. Techniques are gauged by their ends and by their achievements in terms of attaining the end. Expressions are of a less dynamic and active character. To some extent they are essential to the presence of the political entity, though, of course, a sharp line between presence and activization cannot be observed here either. We can only say that the active character of the political sphere is relatively more prominent in the channels of its functional activity than in its status as an entity made manifest in government. Hence it is precisely in modern society, involved in so many activities and agencies, that we may sometimes retain dynasties or personal embodiments of the political entity and sovereignty, something which is impossible on the functional level, where the impersonal character is more prominent. An individual human being, as for instance a monarch, or even an elected president, can be conceived as representing the entity. Thus, at least seemingly, the distinction between the impersonal and the personal aspect of the political entity if blurred, while that distinction is observed — and is bound to be observed — in the instrumental channels of the political sphere.

Summing up this part of our analysis, we may say that power represents the capacity to give orders, while subjection to power amounts to some extent to obeying the orders. The two aspects are interrelated; the continous pursuit of legitimization of power is the search by those holding it for the justification of their capacity, and by those who obey for the explanation of their factual obedience as justified. Weber pointed to this significant aspect when he referred to governments (*Herrschaft*) as an opportunity for order containing defined content, and for obtaining obedience among persons. Our own argument can be viewed as an exposition of those factors which make for correlation between the activity of governing and the activity of obeying. At this point we must underscore that obeying is also an activity and is not only a passive, receptive attitude to be accepted or justified. To be sure there are different aspects of that justification, starting with the awareness of dependence on the establishment of institutions serving ends, and continuing to the shift to expressions which, on the one hand, make the political entity manifest and, on the other, serve that entity. There is both a quantitative and a qualitative difference between particular objectives, such as safety and security, health and employment, and an agency which serves the very position, i.e. cohesion, of the political entity. It is evident that all these aspects are mutually interwoven, and we distinguish between them analytically only.

(9)

Moreover, there is no political entity and no political activity taking place in it and serving it that is not intentional.[6] Intentionalities and intentions may increase in certain historical circumstances; the intensity of their presence may be culturally explained as Claude Lévi-Strauss does in his distinction between 'hot' and 'cold' societies, and as it is presented in anthropological studies, for instance in Margaret Mead's analysis of the generation gap. Even when we accept patterns of the past, what Margaret Mead called 'pre-figurative culture', this is an acceptance and not just an imitation lacking awareness and thus deliberation and intentions as attitudes and acts.

Relations to the past as well as to the future are relations grounded in awareness. While our attitude to the future is commonly characterized as one of anticipation, we lack a term for our broad attitude towards the past, which is not only retention as Husserl called it; for the reference to the past we could perhaps coin the brief and symmetrical term 'postcipation' — echoing the term 'anticipation'. There is no escape from intentions — and, therefore intentionality as such is not a historical phenomenon to be located in changing cultural environments. In this

---

6. On the question of intentionality in social life cf. Margaret Mead: *Culture and Commitment, A Study of the Generation Gap*, published for the American Museum of Natural History Press, by Doubleday, Garden City, New York, 1970; and by Panther, London, 1972; Clark Kerr: *Marshall, Marx and Modern Times, The Multi-Dimensional Society*, Cambridge University Press, Cambridge, 1969; Harvey Wheeler: *The Politics of Revolution*, Glendessary Press, Berkeley, California, 1971. See also the present author's 'The Art of Governing and Intentionality' in *The Human Context*, Vol. VII, 1975, pp. 373-379.

sense political activity is an intentional activity *par excellence*, since it is concerned with the continuous emergence and preservation of human interrelations and their channelling. Naturally, the more activities there are, and the more variegated the social political sphere, the more intentionality is brought into the scope of society and political activities. On this point we can agree with the analysis of Wheeler, who says that the intentional society cannot be achieved effortlessly, like sleep-learning. The intentional society, as he calls it, seeks to become self-aware of its own intrinsic logic of quality and to realize it in politics. We may add that this intentional realization in politics renders the different components of the political sphere more articulate and calls for a continuous awareness, e.g. of the distinction between the aspect of ends and the aspect of position, though in many situations we may be overwhelmed by the functional aspect of politics. We are not touching here on ideological problems, since we are deliberately confining our analysis to phenomenological features of the political sphere. But one aspect of the Marxist legacy has to be explored in the present context in order to round off our analytical exploration.

The impact of Marx's theory on the intellectual climate of the present day, as well as the intrinsic significance of his views, call for a more detailed exploration of this point of our discussion. The more so since that theory — propounding the view that political activity in the orbit established by it is essentially of a secondary character — presents a point of departure, both for a critical analysis and for a reinforcement of the positive arguments presented in the preceding exploration. It is evident that Marx's distinction between human as against political emancipation implies a certain conception of the political realm which indeed was made specific in his writings. In a well-known statement Marx says that every emancipation is a restoration of the human world and of human relationships to man himself. Hence his conception, both from the point of view of the ontological status and historical locus, presupposes what he calls 'man himself', who is an active being. The restoration of his activity implies or calls for the removal of restrictions imposed on man by any external power, which is, in the first place, a political power. Emancipation as restoration of the active man is not only a liberation of man from certain yokes as well as the safeguarding of certain rights to which man is entitled, such as rights in the legal and political spheres or the right to worship. Emancipation amounts to the restoration of the basis of human life, and thus is a liberation of man from his subjection to politics and to governments, since man incorporates within himself both his inherent value and the direction of his activites, which direction is encroached upon, suppressed and curtailed by the political sphere and its built-in hierarchy.

Basically man himself as a self-controlling entity is the total man — 'total' connoting the non-specialized man — capable of performing the whole spectrum of human activities. It is in this sense that Marx's attempt to restore man to his proper status, and to criticize the subjugation of man is, in terms of the history of ideas, a version of the theme of *uomo universale*, since man originally engaged in a variety of activities: hunting in the morning, fishing in the afternoon, etc. without ever becoming a hunter or a fisherman or in any way continually identifying with any specialized activity. The political sphere in general and political emancipation aiming at the establishment of certain human rights are not essentially an attempt in the direction of restoring the human world *qua* redemption of the full creativity of man. Political emancipation is, on the one hand, a reduction of man to his position in society as an indpendent and egotistic individual, and, on the other, an elevation of man as a citizen or as a moral person. Thus political activity, even when it aims at the restoration of human rights, maintains the basic dichotomy within the human realm between man as a egotistic individual and man as a moral person, a realm where morality militates against the egotistic attitudes and tendencies of the individual. Political activity in its historical sense cannot be made to foster the idea of *uomo universale*, precisely because it maintains the split in human reality, widened by the organizational set-up of political reality. The desideratum is to bridge the chasms characteristic of human existence and exploited by the political activity.

Human emancipation which goes beyond political activity is an attempt to give expression to the fullness of human essence by turning man into a social being. As a consequence of this, political power is removed from the human realm once man adopts his position as an abstract citizen, a position circumscribed by the organized character of political activity, leading to a separation between the real man and the abstract citizen. Man is an abstract citizen in the political realm because he participates in a state which is detached from the real essence of man and superimposed on it. As a matter of fact, for Marx the individual man in his everyday life can lead an harmonious existence, both as an individual and as a social being. However, political activity not only brings about a synthesis between the political and the social aspect; it may also lead to a separation of these two aspects of human essence and even to a clash between them. To be sure, in order to pose this synthesis as the fulfilment of human essence, Marx had to assume that man is essentially *ein Gattungswesen*, in order to show that the split between individual existence and social existence is already a split in the human essence. The eventual restoration of that essence is a return to the basic factual and essential predisposition of human essence and activity. Marx had to assume, just the same, that there is bound to be an organization of human beings, since the individual forces as such do not possess an innate propensity to become harmonious forces safeguarding social existence. There is — or will be — an organization of a political character, or, to put it differently, we must distinguish between social and political organizations.[7]

Already at the point we must emphasize the quandary in which Marx finds himself, since he attempts to posit an orbit of the manifestation of human nature which is organized, social, and thus not simply an expression of man's spontaneity. But that orbit is not political, because for him political organization carried the intrinsic meaning of bringing about a hierarchical structure consisting of governors and the governed. Marx says that life in common emerges from the needs and egoism of individuals. Therefore it is not in man's power to decide whether the common life of human beings exists or not or should exist or not. The fact that it is not up to man himself to decide on

7. Karl Marx: *Selected Writings in Sociology and Social Philosophy*, ed. by T.B. Bottomore and Maximilian Ruber, Pelican Books, 1963, p. 241; *The German Ideology*, ed. by R. Pascal, New York, 1947, p. 22. See also the present author's 'Human Emancipation and Revolution', *Interpretation*, Vol. 3/2, 3, 1973, pp. 205ff.

the very existence of life in common has to be understood in
the sense that it is not up to man to decide on this basic issue
by way of reflecting, deciding or deliberating. But Marx is still
in search of a genetic explanation of the common life of man.
Thus he is led to the conclusion that where the emergence of
common life is concerned we find a coalescence of authenticity
and necessity: it is the authentic essence of human nature to
live a common life and at the same time it is necessary for
human beings to live a common life for the sake of the fulfilment of their needs. Still, the political organization amounts
to a separation from human authenticity because in the political
realm the component of compulsion becomes central, and compulsion is opposed to human authenticity. Thus, even when
Marx does not cling to the notion of full spontaneity he rejects
a limine the ingredient of compulsion: human needs are still
a part of human essence, while compulsion is simply an imposition and thus an external factor.

(10)

As we have reiterated, the point of departure of the present
analysis lies in the coexistence of human beings. This is a factual
situation and as such does not call for recourse to human essence
and does not lead to a genetic exploration of itself. If we look
again at the Aristotelian model which identifies coexistence with
the root of human rationality and communication between
human beings, and Marx's attempt to relate coexistence to needs,
we are left in the dark as to the extent to which any of these
'genetic' suggestions can really explain the fact that human beings live together and establish certain relations between them.
Marx's position is certainly a case in point, since though in his
view needs are the explaining factor of human sociability, needs
also explain situations of conflict when — rightly or wrongly —
they become identical with interests. Once the same factor, i.e.
need, is viewed as explaining both human harmony and human
conflict we may wonder, both conceptually and empirically, to
what extent this factor meets its expected purpose as an explaining or genetic motivation for human coexistence, let alone

sociability, in society. It would be hardly justified to assume that spontaneous human needs create sociability, while particularistically interpreted human needs become rigid and separatistic, bringing about conflicts undermining human sociability and imposing one direction of interests by one group of human beings on other human beings and their direction of interests. Hence we may wonder to what extent the genetic explanation adds to the understanding of the political realm, let alone to the explanation of political activity. Once we take coexistence as our point of departure, no distinction can be made at that level between the social component and the political component of human existence. To put it more sharply, there is no justification in viewing political activity merely as a deformation of the social character of human existence, or to view the historical process as aiming at the restoration of the social essence of man through the withering away of political activity since basically that activity does not conform to human essence but dismembers it. This is not to say, as we shall see presently, that the political sphere does not contain an element which can be regarded as the element of interest. Yet there is a difference between considering interests as an ingredient of the political sphere and viewing them as creating that very sphere.

Essentially Marx conceived of the political sphere and political activity as imbued with an instrumental character. Indeed, as we have seen before, there is no doubt that the aspect of instrumentality is present in the political sphere. But there, too, we question the attempt to totalize political instrumentality without viewing it also as related to the presupposition of human coexistence, and as an attempt to make that coexistence only subservient to particular interests, or to put it differently, as an attempt to identify that broad character of the political sphere with its interpretation as coinciding with particular interests. We can ask ourselves at what point does the aspect of particular interests emerge in the political context through exploitation of that context for the cultivation and promotion of particular interests? In the first place it has to be conceptually and empirically recognized that in order to identify exploitation on behalf of particular objectives determined by interests or identical with them, we have to presuppose the political context as instrumental to the promotion of these interests.

Marx's attempt to explain the emergence of the political sphere led him to investigate the motivation underlying that sphere, the motivation which he identified with interests. But once we presuppose the context of human concurrence, we are bound to arrive at the conclusion that human interests do not initiate the political sphere but can be and are only an activizing factor within that sphere. It can be said, for instance, that interests related to economic concernes and objectives bring into the political sphere, based as it is on coexistence and its amplifications, the structure of exchangeability and striving for advantage which is also characteristic of the sphere of work and labour. This is a case where the breadth of the sphere, as a sphere of reality, can absorb within itself structures of a different order, precisely because as a sphere of reality it has enough 'loopholes' into which structures of a different character can infiltrate or penetrate. This combination between coexistence and interests becomes even more prominent when we take another look at the growing intentionality characteristic of the political sphere, which means that interests as motivations guide intentions and intentionalities, eventually guiding policy decisions, functional agencies and by the same token governments. The correlation between motivation and intention is an essential point in the context. But here, too, we have to distinguish between the context of intentionality, which precedes acts of deliberation and guidance, and those very acts as explicit manifestations of decisions or motivations.

An additional question can be raised at this juncture: do interests appeal to human beings solely because of the manipulative character of political activity — this is to a very large extent the model or the presupposition of Marx's theory — or is there a different, though partial, explanation of the impact of interests in the human context? The following might be a reasonable conjecture: interests have a two-fold character — on the one hand they are unintentional guiding forces, and on the other they are intentional. In the sense that they are related to factual operating forces, such as subsistence, interests expressing needs; but in the sense that they are related to calculations or the weighing of alternatives — which in turn can be viewed as means for the satisfaction of needs — they express intentions and evaluations. For Marx interests as urges and interests as calculations were equivalent. In addition, it might be said about the political sphere that since men factually conduct their existence in an inter-human context, they are best left to themselves; since the human context is given, the less intention is introduced into it the better the context will be preserved. According to this mode of reasoning, factual human considerations *qua* interests are both maintaining factors of human coexistence and activating factors within that coexistence and for its sake. At this point, political controversies can be understood as primarily ideological controversies. What is usually called a conservative approach to politics amounts to a reliance on factual motivations, including reliance on the 'hidden hand' of interests, while what is called a progressive or radical interpretation of the political sphere and its ideology amounts rather to a reliance on an intentional intervention in the political sphere. The latter approach to politics presupposes that, given that coexistence is there in the first place, it does not automatically take care of itself but needs a continuing intervention that channels, but does not create it.

(11)

It is necessary to give some further attention to the concept of interest before restating the tension between the given reality of coexistence and the position of interest as a historical factor and as a motivating force, exerting influence, according to Marx, *inter alia*, on the political domain and its concomitant activity. In the context of Marx's analysis as well as in the everyday vernacular we can distinguish between three interrelated components of the notion of interest: (a) the advantage, that is to say, that part of an achievement or reality which is beneficial to the partner or to the agent; (b) related to the first component is the utilitarian aspect, which, as well as the result of the action, contains the motivation to achieve a utilitarian effect from it; the whole is characterized by the fact that eventually the agent finds the situation to his benefit. Although the first and the second aspects are close to each other, the second places a stronger emphasis on the motivation to achieve the utilitarian result, while the first refers only to the factual advantage; (c) the third ingredient is that of possessing a share in an achievement or situation, which means that one's interest amounts to one's participation in the goods or commodities available, or, in other words, the advantage amounts to one's share, or the beneficient outcome of one's action amounts to part of that which will accrue to the agent.

The particular feature of Marx's interpretation of interest should be amplified by certain considerations which can be summed up as follows: (a) interests are related to needs: one has a need for subsistence, and thus one's need for subsistence takes the shape of advantage, utility and participation; (b) though needs can be delineated as belonging to individuals, individual needs still have a common denominator. Therefore, from the point of view of needs, there are groups or classes of human beings objectively motivated by the same needs and thus by the same interests; (c) in this sense needs and interests are the substructure of human behaviour: they express a stratum of reality and motivation which is basic and indelible, precisely because it consists of needs; (d) we are looking for what may be described as an energizing or activating factor in human behaviour and in human reality. The activizing factor is bound to be constituted by needs, because they have an essentially two-fold character — that of causes and that of ends. On the one hand they motivate, and on the other they contain in themselves the direction of their satisfaction, at least on the economic or material level; (e) interests are essentially partial since they refer to the agents, their needs and advantages, as well as to their directedness towards participation in what might be understood in the literal sense of the term as commonwealth or common welfare. Yet there are certain groups of people who are closer to wealth, i.e. the bourgeoise, and other groups who are closer to the common factor of human interaction, i.e. the proletariat. Hence the interest of the proletariat conforms to the interest of the common weal, while the interest of the bourgeoisie coincides with the manipulation of the commenwealth in the interest of the bourgeois class; this manipulation is essentially the political activity.

Having summed up two considerations, that related to the factor of interest in general and that related to Marx's interpretation of it, we may raise some additional critical questions. The first refers to the whole notion of the energizing or activizing factor, having suggested the impact of interest as that energizing factor. Marx had to presuppose that man is a *Gattungswesen*, which can be rendered as an 'entity of a species'. Hence he, too, had to presuppose a kind of an existent community or communality with regard to the position of man. But interestingly enough he preferred to make a statement which we would describe today as related to essence rather than to existence: he referred to the essence of man as an entity of a species and not to his given reality as constituted by the primary coexistence of the plurality of human beings and the continuous interpretation of empirical factors of that coexistence − the interpretation with which we started our analysis of the political activity. In any case, the broad spectrum of community or coexistence is presupposed by Marx. Therefore, interest proper can only refer to activities against the background of community or common essence, and not to causes or factors bringing about the very emergence of the common essence or of the coexistence. Indeed, interests are partial and they are aimed at securing a share within the community or coexistence. Hence on the one hand they presuppose coexistence to start with, and coexistence in which their fulfilment will be integrated, on the other. Partialness is therefore an essential feature of interests. Hence we cannot assume that interests as such contain in themselves a springboard for the leap from partialness to community, let alone universality.

Marx in his criticism called attention to the distinction between the concrete and the abstract by pointing to the socio-economic situation as representing the concrete, and to statehood and political activity as embodying the abstract, whereby the abstract conceals its dependence upon the concrete although it is manipulated by the latter. He took the particular abstractum *qua* political power not only as a detached entity, but as a tool in the service of the concrete lives of the concrete human beings within the state. But once he viewed the position of the state both as abstract and as an instrument subservient to concrete needs or interests, he established the possibility for a conjunction between abstractness and instrumentality. This essential conjunction entails the possibility of going beyond the particular historical encounter, namely, that of the bourgeoisie and the instrumentality of the state. The way can be opened for the working class as well in the direction of taking advantage of the instrumentality of the state for the fulfilment of the needs and interests of that class. The very conjunction between abstractness and instrumentality implies that state and political power, emanating from coexistence and representing it, are, by definition as well as by their historical position, broader than any particular use of the instrumentality by a particular social class. After all, it is one of the advantages of the position of an abstract entity that it can be concretely interpreted in different ways, and therefore applied and employed for different goals, including those dictated by needs and interests. In addition, Marx's criticism was directed against the very position of instrumentality in the human context, because for him, apparently, instrumentality amounts to an estrangement from spontaneous human behaviour as well as from the basic needs that are the ultimate energizing factor and cause of human behaviour. To put it differently, since Marx started with human essence *qua Gattungswesen*, and not with human reality *qua* primary coexistence, he over-emphasized the factor of spontaneity in human essence and its expectations, neglecting the factor of organization. Organization is one of the modes of human coexistence, which is a given fact and as such finds its manifestations, among others, in organization and the techniques pertaining to it. At this juncture Marx was oblivious of the character of human society as a structure of structures, since he assumed, somewhat over-optimistically, the continuity from the entity of the species to inter-human relations as being, at least potentially, harmonious. In the orbit of concrete human existence Marx apparently addressed himself to only one aspect of common existence, which can be described as that of mutuality. Mutuality connotes empirically the exchangeability characteristic of work and its product on the one hand, and the reciprocity of human respect on the other. Since Marx's concern was with basic needs as the ultimate motivating factor, he rightly discerned the aspect of mutuality and reciprocity in the exchange of services or commodities. The political organization was not viewed by him as grounded in human reciprocity, but as an instrument for subjugation or — from the opposite angle — not as an expression of human nature but as something superimposed over that nature. Indeed, at this point we see again that the philosophical distinction between the reference to human essence or the reference to the facticity of human coexistence has far-reaching consequences in the analysis and the evaluation of the political sphere. Political organization does not express mutuality and exchangeability, but the very togetherness and the belonging of those implicated in it. There is a difference between mutuality and togetherness, since the former pertains to inter-human relations, while the latter delineates the boundaries of the society as embodied in the territorial base, lineage, and common language. On the level of mutuality human beings expect something from each other, while on the level of togetherness they are aware of their belonging and are engaged in expressing it. It would be, to use Whitehead's famous phrase, 'a fallacy of misplaced concreteness', to view human existence as confined only to mutuality and to superimpose that mode of human interaction on other modes of it, and most significantly, on the mode of political activity and the realm constituted by it.

Coming back to Marx we may say that Marx, despite, or because of, the fact that he referred to basic human needs as a factor motivating human reality, presented a moralistic model grounded in mutuality and superimposed it on other modes of human existence, which cannot be subsumed under the heading a moral interpretation of the human reality. It is appropriate to quote here a statement of Kant's from his *Perpetual Peace*: 'Given a multitude of rational beings requiring universal laws to their preservation, but each of whom is secretly inclined to exempt himself from them, to establish a constitution in such a way that, although their private intentions conflict, they check each other, with the result that their public conduct is the same as if they had no such intentions.' And further: 'A good constitution is not to be expected from morality, but, conversely, a good moral condition of a people is to be expected only under a good constitution.'[8]

There is a particular dialectical structure to the position of interests in a society and in a political orbit — and this has to be stressed despite the fact that renowned dialecticians have addressed themselves to interests and their impact in social and political life. In terms of political activity and at least one of its goals, it can be said that those advocating interests and pursuing them assume an ambiguous position: they unmask the interests of another group or even individual, while the very unmasking carries with it the meaning of an absence of identity between the interest and those adhering to it on the one hand, and the broad scope of society and the political realm on the other. Interests are unmasked as being embodiments of partialness. Thus by definition and as a matter of fact, they cannot be viewed as identical with the political sphere and its dynamic character. In other words, the process of unmasking presupposes the notion and the goal of coexistence, and, dialectically, places that goal above interests and the justification of the groups adhering to them. It is at this point that we find one of the justifications for the emergence of ideologies in political life, if we understand here ideology as a deliberate formulation of a certain intention, related to the political sphere and its goal. Interests, therefore, lend themselves to occupy the position of focal points of social criticism from both sides: those who tend to identify the interests with the whole structure of the society and those who, by unmasking the unjustified identification, propose a different structure of the society which will overcome the inherent particularism of interests.

This dialectical structure of the controversy and even of the clash centering around the position of interests in the political orbit again makes prominent the two-fold position of statehood and government. The fact that a state or a government are instruments subservient to interests does not imply that instruments as such are to be unmasked. What is unmasked is the particular relationship between this or that partial interest and

8. *Perpetual Peace*, included in *Immanuel Kant on History*, edited, with an introduction by Lewis White-Beck, Library of Liberal Arts, Indianapolis, 1963, pp. 112-223.

the particular relationship between this or that partial interest and the *quasi* neutrality of states and governments. Again, this unmasking is meant to bring into the concept of instrumentality embodied in statehood and governments a different subservience to different interests intended to change the factual situation as well as to bring about a conformity, or at least a proximity, between interests and the collectivity of statehood and governments. This is so since the latter are basically meant to refer to togetherness and coexistence, and not to segments and partial sectors. The very appeal to the institutional manifestation of togetherness is therefore an axis of political controversies as well as a focus of political ideologies and their pragmatic manifestations. To be sure, the tension between partialness and collectivity is not confined to the aspect of interests in the sense explored up to this point. The well-known story about the group of soldiers addressing an assembled mass, proclaiming 'we are the representatives of the people', and the mass answering 'we are the people' is a case in point. Though the whole notion of representation and representatives intrinsically carries the reference to those who are represented and thus does not create a sector of partialness inside the society but a symbolic level of the total society, pragmatically it can just the same create the tension between partialness and totality. Thus the continuous appeal to the wholeness of the society is implied in this mode of tension as well.

We can revert at this point to one of the ideological transformations of these different tensions related to the notion of 'minimum of government'. We can understand that notion as reflecting the fear that government as such if aggrandized will become a partial sector within the society and *vis-à-vis* the society, and thus will turn out to be an embodiment of partial interests. On the other hand — and this is at least one aspect of the modern development of social life — if interests are left to themselves and the government becomes or is an instrument subservient to them, one of the ways of overcoming the partialness of government as explicating the partialness of interests is to amplify and reinforce the position of government as such, since theoretically government appears as a manifestation of the all-embracing togetherness and not of a particular sector and a particular interest. In terms of unmasking, it can be said that one of the ideological controversies may center around that issue, namely that the notion of minimum government, though allegedly meant to serve society as a whole, pragmatically serves definite interests within society. It has to be observed that we are simply attempting here, without taking any side, to delineate the *loci* of ideological controversies and their rationale in terms of the basic structure of the political sphere and political activity.

However, the dialectical position of interests in the social and political spectrum can be seen from an additional point of view: interests drive those who adhere to them in the direction of changing the structure of the society, not by amplifying the norm of coexistence as the superior norm of the political realm, but by trying to establish an interest through acquiring a share in the goods and commodities already rendered by the society. The particular clash between interests amounts eventually to an aspiration to gain a share in the structure as it stands. Here, too, the tension between partialness and wholeness is present and even tangible, though the wholeness is not now distinguished as a goal of political activity, but is a present locus for participation *qua* share in the socio-political realm as it exists. In the first case the dynamic character of interests and the concomitant ideologies amounts to the projection of the wholeness as the embodiment of coexistence. In the second case the motivation by interests directs their pursuit towards a different distribution of that which is already available. But in the second case, as in the first, the reference to coexistence is present and perhaps paradoxically even more so than in the first case. In the first case to coexistence is projected, in the second case it is taken for granted.

Be this as it may, we encounter here, in terms of our analysis of the position of interests in the political sphere and of interests as motivations for political activity, the particular dialectical tension between partialness and togetherness. Coming back to our point of departure, we have to reiterate that togetherness is not invented *en route* to the particular pursuits of political goals. It is a permanent coordinate of political activity.

Here again we come to the conclusion that the political sphere, the activity accompanying it, and the reference to it — are projected by human beings out of their awareness of belonging, inasmuch as belonging is a point of departure and not an utopian goal. The political sphere is accompanied by a permanent awareness of its inherent paradox, which is the paradox of togetherness: unless togetherness is expressed in institutions or in governments embodying the capacity of compulsion, even primary togetherness is not safeguarded. Togetherness is there, and the awareness of its weakness is there too. The political sphere is therefore characterized by this continuous attempt to overcome the weakness of the very point of departure of the sphere of politics. The point of departure is not invented or artificially set up. This being so, it does not preclude the continuous intentionality of the political sphere and even calls for that intentionality. We grant the facticity of human togetherness and also grant that this togetherness is both a potentiality and an actuality, which has to be constantly activized. The power-character of statehood is, from this point of view, not a mere accident or an embodiment of a partial interest. It is a projected extension of the basic stratum of coexistence or togetherness. That stratum in turn does not contain a protective device of its own. Therefore, the projection and the extension go on indefinitely. This being so, the instrumentality of political power is not predetermined in the direction of any of the divergent interests, since these interests impose themselves on the projected character of the instrumentality and therefore presuppose it. Compulsion inherent in political power, which in turn is sanctioned or legitimized, e.g., by the legel system, appears as a tacit 'insurance policy': human beings devise a protective instrument in case they do not conform to the expected conduct and its supposed standard, i.e. coexistence and togetherness. This is not a contract, since we do not suggest a step from the stage of isolated individuals to that of togetherness, or, put differently, the tacit insurance already presupposes the togetherness and presupposes reflection, experience, anticipation related to the given togetherness and its momentum. Again, one of the possible arguments within the political orbit, related as it is to devices of compulsion, is that compulsion is used as a *prima ratio* instead of an *ultima ratio*. This possible argument and its ideological expressions refer to basic coexistence or togetherness, claiming that if those are presupposed there is no need to start out immediately from the level of compulsion. Such a start amounts to the opposite basic presupposition of war of all against all which can only be prevented by compulsion.

Coming back to Marx's position we may say that his concept of universal man led him to an assumption that there would be a single-layered human actuality instead of conceiving human actuality as a structure of different components as well as of different levels of activities. Even when we accept the notion of radicalism as a return to the roots — which is after all a metaphor — we may still wonder what and where the roots are: are they grounded in the position of the individual agent embodying human essence, or are they grounded in a coexistence which is a fact and may or may not be an extension of human nature? In any case, we are led back to the notion that political acitivity takes place within history and not beyond it, neither at a point preceding it nor at a point replacing it. Political activity is factual and its justification lies in the continuous reference to that facticity as well as in the continuous attempt to translate it into a norm, without erasing the facticity itself.

At this point we are led to an exploration of the nature of moral activity, which, to say the least, is not merely factual and whose normative character is not only an extension or amplification of a factual background.

(13)

In a sense a phenomenological exploration of the political order tends to explore the permanent features of that order. Yet since that order is situated in history — and that situation implies also an exposure to historical changes — it is proper to deal with the impact of one major change on the political activity, i.e. the impact of technology. We turn to that topic first by describing its context in the political order as such.

The previously introduced distinction between the expressive and the functional aspects of the political activity, the latter embodied in government or governance, leaves the functional channel open to what might be described as historical changes, preparing the ground for the absorption of some of these changes into the direction of the activity of governing. That direction, though grounded in the functional perspective, may go beyond functional considerations. A case in point is the issue of the impact of technological changes on the political order and the activity emanating from it. Here we encounter the relevance of historical change for political activity, whether these changes are of an ideological character — as for instance the ideology of progress — or related to a contemporary orientation such as technology. Since the context of the foreign relations of a political order is of both an expressive and functional character the relevance of technology to foreign relations may be seen more as being relevant to the component of dominance than that of embodying the underlying cohesion of the political system. There is of course a feedback of one channel of activity to the other.

One additional preliminary comment is appropriate at this juncture. In exploring political activity we shall lay stress on the issue of the elements of the political order as such. The shift towards the functional aspect of the political activity also raises the question as to what extent that shift may eventually lead to an overemphasis of the functional direction. To some extent the shift itself is due to the exposure of the political order to historical change. Once that exposure is pertinent it brings about a concurrent exposure to the changes of content and orientation occurring in history. The impact of technology on political activity is a case in point.

(14)

We come back to two descriptions — one of politics and one of technology. *Politics* here represents the set of means by which man puts to use the forces inherent in his social organization. In this sense, politics also denotes the struggle of men for their share of social power. *Technology*, on the other hand, represents the set of means by which men put the forces and laws of nature to use. Hence, we may restate our problem as being the effect of man's relation with nature upon relations among human beings and the order they create on that level.

The first point we shall take up is the social influence of technology upon politics, an influence which may be termed indirect. In virtue of the influence it exerts upon society, technology also affects the exercise of social power and authority. A convenient instance of social changes caused by technology and having widespread political repercussions is afforded by the social consequences of the technological innovations of the nineteenth century, beginning with the Industrial Revolution and the growth of urban society. Technological changes have altered the composition of the ruling classes and brought new elements to power. The advance of technology has become a factor both within government and in the struggle over it. Since man's existence rests upon his relations with nature, any changes in these relations will perforce leave their mark upon the internal human system. In other words, politics — insofar as it is a human affair — is part of man's existence in general; and since man's existence is rooted, *inter alia*, in the system that lies between him and nature, changes in this system are bound to show up in the so-to-speak autonomous human system.

Moreover, the set of means that mediate between man and nature is liable to become a political asset — that is, a holding in the hands of a social or ruling force — and the object of struggle for partial or complete control. The resources by means of which man's existence is changed an improved can also become political assets. In the same way that technology influences the course of politics, the course and structure of politics influence technology: they transplant it from the realm of relations between man and nature — to which our definition ascribed it — to the internal human realm. Thus technology influences politics in two ways: it reorganizes the political forces and it becomes a political asset. On the one hand, its influence is causal, while on the other its influence is that of a much sought-for agent of power.

In addition to the indirect social influence of technology on politics, we find a *psychological* relationship between these two spheres, and we have already dealt with that aspect. The very relation between human existence and technology is rooted in a fundamental aspect of human reality: man must rely upon instruments to satisfy the requirements of his subsistence. A set of elaborate and delicate tools is no more than an extension of primitive utensils: both are the creations of tool-making and tool-using man. There is, however, one qualitative difference between simple utensils and technological tools, properly speaking. Technology, as we have described it, is characterized by the fact that it itself is the product of technological means. Technology was not created by man with his bare hands and capacity: one technology produces another. There is an ever-present barrier between man and the system to which he is related. This, in turn, standardizes the products of technology — which leads to far-reaching economic consequences which we shall not discuss, restricting ourselves to the political effects proper.

Man's relation to technology gives rise to certain expectations. If the aim of technology is to better human existence and make it more comfortable, it is man's desire of comfort that is one of the driving forces behind technology. Technology patently proves to man that his desire for comfort is realizable. Technological achievements give rise to aspirations related to further achievements of the same sort, and then proceed to sharpen and focus the needs which these achievements can satisfy. What is more, the widened participation in the wielding of social power and order does not only mean participation in government, but also the sharing of the achievements of society and humanity. In the reality of the technological civilization, this does not only imply the control of the means of production — as is usually intimated — but also participation in the control of the means of improving human existence, that is, of the achievements of technology. Another aspect of this issue is well illustrated by the technological society: the aspiration to share the achievements of technology can supplant the aspiration to share the control over the means of production, because man's satisfaction lies in the fact of sharing drives and partaking in the technological determinants of life. In other words, technological reality influences socio-political drives, determines them, and fashions them in the image of technology. This reality is liable to deflect one's aims and aspirations from the re-organization of the basic social forces — for example, of the ownership of the means of production — to the wish to become part of the technological order as it stands and the demand that the achievements of technology be available and accessible to all. Thus the achievements of technology indirectly influence the demands of men and, insofar as its aim is the satisfaction of human demands, the sphere of politics as well. The outcome is rather simple and empirically encountered: the worker would rather buy an automobile and television set than have a share in the ownership of the means of production.

This development has influenced the workers' movement, revealing the antagonism between its two primary aims: to free man by making society autarchic over the means to its subsistence, and to improve the worker's actual human status. It assumed that these two aspirations were compatible in two senses: in a positive sense, because the liberation of man necessarily implies the liberation of the worker from his misery; and in a negative sense, because the sufferings of the worker are an offshoot of the basic oppression of man typified in the fact that society is not master over the means of production. The tension between these two aspirations has always existed, yet technological civilization has brought it to a head.

It may also be said that technological civilization has generated an illusion of achievement; for in times of mass unemployment technological achievements will be of no avail. However, illusions can constitute social forces and political factors of no mean importance. For one thing, the *perpetuum mobile* of the technological orbit breeds a reality of constant change while kindling faith in the advent of achievements that will not be mere objective achievements of technology, but will serve the individual — that is, will maintain his standard of living.

It is not enough, however, to deal with the psychological influence of technology on politics from the point of view of this change in aspirations. Were it not for technology, the idea of a welfare state would never have been born. Actually, there are two sides to the idea of the welfare state. On the one hand, society must help man by seeing to it that the ground conquered by technology should not remain desert, or occupied by the privileged few, but be settled by all mankind. The state is called upon to mediate between the level of civilization as a whole and the level of the individual. The welfare state is the mediator between actual human existence and the objective range of technological civilization. The other aspect of the welfare state that bears witness to the influence of technology on politics is man's demand that society and its institutions should act in accordance with the constitutive logic of technology. Society and its institutions are called upon to improve human existence and raise its standards in the same way as technology does. In other words, the *raison d'être* of technology is transferred from the realm of objects and tools to the realm of society and its institutions. Man measures his environment by a technical-utilitarian yardstick. He does this not only in relation to man-made reality — that is, the world of technology — but also to human reality proper i.e. society and its institutions. Here, too, man's demands are formed by technology.

To sum up, technology's direct influence on politics is double: (1) it has widened the scope of politics, by increasing the number of participants in a sphere destined to improve man's existence; (2) but it has also narrowed its scope, by concentrating man's interest on the demand to improve his life and by giving him a yardstick according to which many aspects of his existence are evaluated by technological criteria.

(15)

The indirect influence of technology on politics is even more pronounced than we have so far suggested. Technological reality brings about a human reality of equality in style. Let us draw, in broad lines and for the sake of this analysis, the distinction between three types of inequality: (1) inequality in personal power, be it physical or mental; (2) inequality of ancestry and pedigree; and (3) inequality in affluence. Until the technological civilization prevailed, it was more or less clear that inequality in one of its three categories — and *a fortiori* in all three — leads to inequality in actual human life, in man's style, the opportunities offered him, and so forth. This is not to say that technological civilization has replaced inequality, or removed the essential roots of human inequality. However, technological civilization does make possible the emergence of a realm of human facets characterized by equality, against the background of an inequality no different from what it was, or even more manifest. What is it that has made this process possible?

The technological civilization brings about a certain style of life built around the instruments it provides and the order it establishes. This civilization's ultimate criterion of style of life is comfort. It surrounds man with a multitude of devices, and through them creates a way of life that man accepts because of their very presence. It abolishes habits and ways of life rooted in history or mores, and introduces a style of uniformity. This uniformity of style creates an outwardly human equality. Men are given the opportunity to evaluate and comprehend their life, not only on the basis of the inequality between one person and his fellow man but also by means of the vista of equality that unfolds before them in virtue of their common relation to one system of instruments. This is an atmosphere for the growth of a complex psychological reaction: instead of paying attention to inequality, we tend to fix our gaze upon equality. For instance, even though John may be of privileged ancestry, and extremely rich, there is no difference between his actual style of life and my own, although I am not of priviliged ancestry, nor am I affluent. This intervening reality of the technological world gives birth to an egalitarian psychology, rooted in the existence of egalitarian appearances. Equality is no longer grounded metaphysically in the idea of man having been made in the image of God or in the idea of the rights of man *qua* man. Rather, equality is based on the empirical reality of the confrontation of man and instruments, of the general call for these instruments, and of the style brought about by their existence and use.

This egalitarian frame of mind brings about a particular behaviour. He who adopts this way of thinking usually imputes simplistic motives to politicians. He does not hold an image of them as having superhuman qualities and powers, as bearing a special halo. Fundamentally, there is much in common between him and those who occupy high political positions, precisely in appearance.

We may sum up this discussion of the indirect influence of technology upon politics by confronting two sets of matters: those that belong to the public sphere and the domain of the individual, on the one hand, and those appertaining to the end results of production and consumer products, on the other. Technology influences politics, for insofar as the end results of production are products of technology, heavy machinery and the like become assets of contestable domination. Technology thus affects the public domain, influencing politics *qua* control of the public domain. Technology penetrates into the realm of the individual by means of the various consumer instruments that it designs, thereby creating a style of life, determining responses, evaluations, and ideals. In the long run, these are destined to be reflected in the public domain controlled by politics, a control guided by certain human demands.

(16)

However, technology has left its imprint on the realm of politics itself, and this we call the *direct* influence of technology upon politics. In a way, at present we find ourselves in an historical situation where this influence has not yet made itself fully felt, although we can already sketch some of its lines of development.

If we regard politics as containing the management of the affairs of society, the influence of technology on politics would be first and foremost in the process of management. Technology is one of the processes that increase and intensify the bureaucratic character of the modern state and its institutions, as well as that of the public bodies struggling for supremacy in the state. The modern state is characterized by the increasing power of bureaucracy. Two of the main reasons for this are: (1) bureaucracy represents the applied science of management — that is, it represents the technical capacity and the knowledge of the proper means of organization; (2) bureaucracy represents the social stratum that identifies itself with the interests of the all-embracing state, as opposed to the conflicting sectoral interests within the state. To take a trivial example: the process represented by bureaucracy tends to accrue various office machines — that is, it tends to blend objective, impersonal tools, namely technological machines, with manpower. For instance, the bureaucratic machinery requires varied and complex machines that compile the results of elections and population movements, including advanced electronic computers. This very dependence of the political machine upon technology strengthens the latter, both in social prestige and in actual power. The increase in prestige follows from the fact that people usually tend to hold in esteem those who can operate delicate instruments that are not within general reach. The actual power of the political machine increases as a function of the skill of its staff in using and operating complex technological tools insofar as the administration, to this or that degree, gains a monopoly over certain types of information and ability. This monopoly manifests itself also in the salaries of those who have technical capacities. The penetration of technological tools and achievements increases the tendency of administration and the political process towards bureaucratization. This increase is not caused only by the ambition of those who hold power, but also by objective factors treasured by all, even though not all approve of the social and human consequences of these valued factors.

In other words, ambition is encouraged by an objective factor, which is to serve human ends, including the aid of fortifying government. Since technology is to some extent neutral as regards human aims, it is capable of serving them according to the technology introduced into the systems created. Thus it can serve bureaucratic trends insofar as bureaucracy holds in its hands the physical and organizational means which require technological tools and make their operation possible. It is, so to speak, adapted to the objective trends leading to an increasing use of technological instruments. However, in so doing, it strengthens its standing within life as a whole. The functional ownership of the instruments by the personnel — that is, their use and operation — is at times analogous to the economic ownership of the means of production by this or that group of people. What is more, it is because of technology that this functional ownership is often more important than legal economic ownership, as inscribed in official registers. In the technological realm there is a clear decision for operative domination rather than formal ownership, and in this sense the process is preferred over the static conservation of property. This general trend also brings about the propitious hour for political forces representing the levels of operation within the political process, that is, the forces of personnel and bureaucracy.

(17)

However, in modern reality the influence of technology makes itself felt — or, more exactly, has begun to make itself felt — also at the other end of the political process, at the level of the simple man, or the elector. We may say, as people often do, that from the moment a political process as important as the election of a candidate for an important political position of the state is brought to the homes of every man and child, this political process becomes clear; its halo disappears. The particular atmosphere in which it used to take place and which used to give it so much prestige is taken away from it. From this point of view, the same egalitarian tendency noted above as an attribute, or corollary, of technological reality, appears again. Some add that the visibility of the political process is an assurance against intrigues, which must characteristically be woven in the inner chambers. We cannot say that TV abolishes secret meetings. Yet there is a grain of truth in this view of the so-to-speak 'moralizing' influence of the technological reality upon the political process.

The penetration of TV into the public sphere of politics is in fact the penetration of an instrument designed for the use of the individual in the private sphere into the public sphere. This penetration brings non-political influences to bear upon politics, and they enter its realm by virtue of its dependence upon the individual and his taste. When a political figure or a person with political aspirations is discussed, his effect before a TV camera is noted — that is, his appearance is taken into account. The medium of visual telecommunication occasions meetings which are, so to speak, unmediated visual contacts between two human beings. In spite of the immense difference between the marketplace of Athens and today's vast and densely populated countries, we may say that in this technological modern world there is something of that unmediated contact characteristic of the ancient world. In the long run, this must have a direct political effect. Let us point out some ways in which this penetration of technology into politics influences the latter:

1. First of all is the influence on the primitivization of man's perception. Man will actually want to *sense* political events and

personalities. In the absence of such a possibility, which would bring these near to the body, he will rest content with seeing them with his eyes, which at any rate bring things and people closer to the personal realm than the modality of hearing, and *a fortiori* more than reading the newspaper, let alone a book. The paradox is that technology, which is the fruit of man's capacity of abstraction, will in the end nurture trends toward the tangible; reflection may be replaced by perception.

2. The appearance of events and personalities within the individual's visual area increases the importance of publicity as a weapon in the political arena. In a way, this physical concreteness will diminish the value of ideas and principles, which — unfortunately — do not permit visual transmission and will increase the value of personal attraction and the publicity given to the man on view. Moreover, from this aspect, the penetration of technology into politics is also liable to lower the standards of political life. Here, again, we find technology working at cross-purposes with its own essence: technology, a non-personal realm, works hand in hand with the tendencies that stress the personal component in politics, and helps them overpower the non-personal and conceptual elements in social life.

3. Nevertheless, technological means increase the anonymous individual's influence. By keeping track of the course of events, he indirectly influences it. All must take him into account, flatter his taste and approach his standards. The technology that penetrates into politics introduces the anonymous individual into it. It is true that the anonymous individual pays a very high price for this influence — that is, the price of lowering the *niveau* of the realm which he influences. Nevertheless, his strong influence is not a mere consequence of his existence, but is rather a result of his dependence upon technology, which in turn increases his influence on politics in the measure that it lowers its *niveau*. This, too, is a tension characteristic of the rhythm of the technological realm as a whole.

4. We can point out this influence of technology upon the political reality from another side as well: it is a commonplace that direct democracy is impossible in large nations and densely populated countries, where only representative democracy is possible. However, the penetration of technology into politics creates a

sort of substitute for direct democracy. It is true that not the entire electorate can participate directly in decisions, for these are taken by representatives — and in this sense it is still the principle of representation that underlies modern political life. Yet technology does make possible another sort of participation: *observer-participation* without *decision*, that is, a non-active participation. However, the influence of the individual is also based upon his physical presence, even when it does not express itself in active participation in the course of happenings and decisions. It is the presence itself that becomes a factor of political importance.

5. We witness one of the political manifestations of mass society. Mass society diminishes the value of the individual, it weighs him down with the burden of anonymity. Yet the individual — often desperately — tries in many different ways to escape from the anonymity from which there is no evasion. Over and over again, the story of the man who burnt a temple to have his name go down in history is repeated in our mass society. Of course, today people do not burn temples, because they are not as prominent, but they do strange things, and even try to go down Niagara Falls in a barrel. However, the dialectic of the mass society leads to the elevation of the political status of the anonymous individual, who stays at home and stares at his TV screen. Man in his very anonymity becomes a political entity, but on one condition: that he remains part of the masses. Where the individual is most insignificant, there his influence grows, without removing him from the cadres of mass society. In other words, technology nurtures the inherent trends of mass society, while awarding the prize demanded by the individual for his membership in the masses.

Yet, within this process of the accentuation of the individual, he pays a toll. Politics invades his privacy: he is forced at home to be a spectator of the course of public happenings. His home is overrun by the public domain. It is then, and only then, that the individual can influence the public domain. He does not go out into the public domain as in one of the direct democracies of the Ancient World: the public domain comes to him. At first blush, this seems to represent the utmost in comfort, yet actually this means the abolition of privacy, the abolition of the home as man's castle. The home in a mass society should constitute the individual's last fortress against mass society. Yet the anonymous individual becomes an influential political element, since he falls into the clutches of the political domain even when he is in his own, private, domain.

This corrosion of the private by the public domain is even more crucial in view of the character of political life, as it is ostentatiously displayed by technological instruments. Political life must perforce be dramatic, otherwise it would not answer the demands of TV appearances. This dramatic aspect cannot be produced by a conflict between ideas; it tends therefore to be based on a conflict between persons. In the absence of this kind of drama, the attention of the anonymous individual will not be attracted, and he will not turn his thoughts to the public domain. Technology determines the shape of politics, and it is the taste of the consumer that determines what technology will bring to his home.

(18)

Speaking about 'decision', we must distinguish between the act of decision and the concept the decision is about. This distinction runs parallel to the distinction between the act of thinking and the content the act is directed to. Decision is an occurrence *qua* action and as such cannot be totally derived from the content it refers to, as the act of thinking cannot be totally derived from the content the act is concerned with. In the realm of decision, we have to point out an additional component, namely the component of will, which connotes the capacity for the momentum of action, the decision connoting the leap to action or else setting the direction the action is about to take. The machine does not decide, because the machine is conditioned or programmed in the first place. Thus the machine is related to contents and does not possess an attitude toward the contents — decision connoting here an attitude leading to action for the sake of arriving at the content. The act of decision is outside the rational realm and thus cannot be invested in a machine, which is in possession of rational contents. The decision is pre-methodical and thus cannot be inherent in a machine which is methodically programmed. To speak about decisions of machines or of computers is from this point of view to use a metaphoric or anthropomorphic language. These linguistic usages should be avoided whenever we are committed to precision.

What is intended by way of an application to the realm of politics seems to be this: within the realm of politics, clearly including strategy and economics, there always seem to be several possible avenues of action. The information provided by the machine shows the relevant data. According to these date, either human beings decide what avenue they are to take to implement the objectives they set for themselves, or else a machine will push the button and start action in a certain direction. Yet in the latter case there is no decision proper but again only programming, that is to say, the way from information, made available, to action is a way from data presented to pushing the button, which again is metaphorically described as action. It is action in the sense that it has human consequences and the human consequences are here not due to natural — for example, meteorological, volcanic, and so on — occurrences. But it is not an action in the sense of being set by an act of facing a situation and creating the direction of action by a momentum of will and decision. Hence decisions about objectives — for example, the independence of a country or of producing durable or consumers' goods — are decisions taken by human beings who according to these primary decisions program the machines they are constructing. The machine provides information about the conditions in which the objectives are to be implemented or it provides information about the eventual outcomes of the implemented decision.

Even if we assume that technology cannot penetrate the act of decision, and will not replace it with a technical operation, we cannot conclude that a decision can be taken in a vacuum, without involving calculations or thought. These are influenced by technology and its instruments. What is more, technology is not only a set of means: it has also become a set of aims, in reference to the indirect influence of technology upon human demands and ideals. It seems that decisions — however technology-resistant — do occur within a frame moulded to this or that extent by technology. We notice here the impact of technology on the very substratum of action as well as the limits of that impact. Action ceases to be 'pure' action and thus, strangely, the relation between action and reflection emerges again in the context.

We face here the problem of the relations between technology and politics. Politics itself is a realm of means in the hands of man in view of organizing and managing his life. Technology is a system of means that can serve politics while penetrating into it and directly influencing it. However, indirectly influencing politics, it is liable to become more than a system of means and be perceived as standing on the level of ends. Its very existence represents progress, the betterment of man's way of life, the domination of nature, and other such assets that can be perceived as aims instead of being considered as means. Technology, man's right hand in the domination of nature, can become an aim of man from the point of view of his own existence. Traditional sociology used to speak of the enslavement — inherent in alienation — of man to his products, and Marx's sociology followed this view. However, the main question is: how can this enslavement of man to himself, that is, to his products, occur? Can this enslavement come about without the fundamental background of man's authoritarianism in general and without his will to rule the world of nature in particular? Is it not the very will to power that creates and prepares the ground for technology's domination of man, in the sense of determining man's aims of life? In other words, had man not based his life upon the categories of ruler and ruled, the ruled could not have become ruler. The relation of domination can only occur within a system where this relation is at all possible — that is, in general, in an authoritarian system, which connotes here a style of existence and not only a political style. In this, politics has influenced technology but not the other way around. Authority and power are political concepts. Political man marks the technological realm with his authoritarian attitude; technology rules over him, because he creates the authoritarian temper in general and forces himself and his world into the authoritarian mould. Technological development as it stands is a function of this intensification of man's authoritarianism, both in relation to nature and in relation to his fellow-men. The authoritarian drive in man has become the technological drive; it feeds technology, makes its progress possible and forces countries and nations to invest the best of their manpower, their best minds, and a great deal of their resources in the progress of technology.

The basic question, for man and not only for politics, is whether this is the only way to nurture the progress of technology; whether it is necessary that the authoritarian drive and it alone should feed technology. We have not yet tried other alternatives, and no other alternatives are yet in view. It is, clear, however, that another alternative would be tied to a different conception of the nature of man, and to a different conception of politics, as holding in check the human power organized in society, and not as its discharge and intensification. This issue obviously has a bearing on the nature of the moral sphere and the activity related to it.

(19)

The practical order is a partial order — not only because it co-exists within one social orbit together with other orders, but also because it faces a political order outside its own sphere of belonging. Hence we have to refer to the aspect of relations between different political orders i.e. to foreign policy. It is clear that foreign policy gives a strong impetus to the developments of technology in our time; first and foremost to military technology, and in its wake to non-military. What is the fundamental relation between foreign policy and technology?

The trait that characterizes modern foreign policy — and perhaps not only modern — is its aim of preserving the power and authority of the societies involved. In this realm there is one striking identification: the existence of the society or the state is conceived as depending upon its power. Power is said to preserve the existence of the society, the nation, or the state. This appears even before we discuss another aspect of foreign policy, namely, the aspect of the expansion of power: the expansion or preservation of existence by means of the expansion of power. In this matter there is a notable difference between foreign policy and interior policy: interior policy controls the power within society — the power which is a result of the very existence of society. In foreign affairs we find a separation — conceptual, of course — between existence and power; power is represented not as an attribute of existence but rather as a means to the preservation and protection of this existence, since the existence is considered to be endangered by the threat arising from the existence of another society or state. This characterization of the aspect of power as instrumental reveals foreign policy as a realm whose rhythm and activity is similar to the rhythm and activity of the realm of technology. A policy which is alert to the means for protecting its existence, and develops both power and authority, becomes sensitive to technology which provides man with means of subsistence and means for the increase of his power. Yet here, too, we find the transition that characterizes the relationship between politics and technology: technology, whose first and foremost interest seems to be man's domination of nature, finds its place within politics, which deals with social existence.

However, the relation between technology and foreign policy has another aspect: the very grounding of human relations upon their external facet is expressed and crystallized in foreign policy as the reduction of human relations to an authoritarian structure of relations. Externality is the basis of authoritarianism, which in turn is the background for the absorption of technology and its development. Technology does not rely upon the technical capacity alone, but also on the basic human background — that is, the background of external human relations — which is a sort of prior social condition for the development of technological capacity.

(20)

The aspect which we have identified sharpens the decisive question: technological achievements are great human achievements, a manifestation of hidden human capacities, of man's ability to listen to, to decode, and to imitate the course of nature, even if the course of nature is not easily understood. The technological phenomenon is a revelation of man's capacity, and not only a manifestation of man's drive for domination. Can there be a use of technology and its development not based on man's will to dominate nature, which would overflow and suffuse the realm of the relations between man and his fellow man — a technology that would manifest man's innate creative capacity? This in a certain sense is a political question. Yet it surpasses politics in its breadth, for it deals with the way of man in general. To refer to man in general means that technology is conceived as one and only one emanation of human creativity; negatively speaking, it amounts to a denial that technology can be the general norm for human creativity in all its diverse expressions.

The justification for viewing technology as only one expression of human creativity presupposes (1) the understanding of human nature as capable of creativity, or as not being confined to the absorption of that which is only given or encountered; (2) the understanding that universal human creativity may have expressions beyond the technological expression. These different expressions have different principles of operation. Accordingly, they may and should be evaluated according to their internal principles. Linguistic expression, for example, has a different principle from that operating in technology, being evaluated by the criterion of expression and communication and not by that of organization and production.

We encounter here not only a metaphysical question as to the nature of human creativity and the map of its various expressions as activities, but we touch on a question which is relevant for the survival of technology itself. Technology presupposes the rational capacity of man, this capacity expressing itself in science, especially mathematical science. The question inevitably arises: would a human being totally conditioned by technology or else creating technology only (leaving aside the impossibility of such a situation because the creator of technology would still be a linguistic being) be in the position of creating even technology? Is there a self-production of technology out of technology's internal resources only? Or does the reproduction of technology presuppose a human creativity which among other channels can also have the technological, but need not necessarily have them or need not be confined to them?

The impact of technology on politics seems to confront us with these fundamental questions. They again presuppose the distinction between thinking and doing, since they presuppose the rationality of man and its impact on actions structured as an order of technology. By the same token these questions lead to an exploration of the moral activity — and even amplify its significance in the spectrum of the relation between reflection and action.[9]

9. Dennis Gabor in his book *The Mature Society*, Secker & Warburg, London, 1972, deals with issues related to the social impact of modern technology. The present author deals with various aspects of human creativity in his book *Man and His Dignity*, The Magnes Press (?), The Hebrew University, Jerusalem, 1983, pp. 49ff.

CHAPTER SEVEN

MORAL ACTIVITY

(1)

The emphasis placed on coexistence in our previous exploration may be understood as already implying 'moral action'. Moral action is often understood as taking place between human individuals, and thus by its nature is a facet of coexistence. Therefore it has, to say the least, an affinity with political activity. Hence the question arises about the particular character, if any, of moral activity, once an inter-human context is already present on the level of political activity. This issue may perhaps serve as a point of departure for our next step: an attempt to analyse the *differentia specifica* of the moral sphere from the position of the activity involved.

Let us start with the following observation: In the political sphere, and from the point of view of the activity taking place in it and addressing itself to it, the inter-human context is a primary fact. We acknowledge this fact and make this acknowledgement the axis of political activity. Yet the question may arise: is the acknowledgement pertaining between different human beings only an acknowledgement of the factual encounter between them; is this acknowledgement only the realistic recognition of the plurality of human beings who are encompassed by a common framework? Or is the recognition perhaps something more than a yielding to facts? Is the recognition perhaps also a recognition of a basic ontological affinity between human beings in their humanity, in addition to the recognition of the differences between empirical human beings belonging to the same framework of coexistence?

If this first reflection is valid, from the point of view of our attempt to approach the exploration of moral activity, then two concomitant aspects become prominent: political activity starts with the awareness of belonging, while moral activity may start with the awareness of affinity, of mutual recognition as individuals, and not necessarily as individuals implicated in networks of political affiliation and coexistence. Political activity is by definition, at least from its point of departure, a partial activity addressed to the given lines of belonging *qua* space, language and lineage, while moral activity is, from its very beginning, of a universal character, since it addresses itself to the individual encountered, whether or not he shares with us the — limited — common ground out of which the political sphere emerges and which the political sphere cultivates. The recognition of individuals as such is therefore the new perspective introduced by moral activity, which takes individuals out of any given framework, attempts to create relationships between them, and leads to deeds grounded in these relationships which are of an interindividual character and therefore not limited by and to any given contexts. The introduction of the individual dimension, which appears parallel to the introduction of the universal dimension, seems, at this stage of our analysis, to be the first component of the moral perspective and of the activity prompted by it.

At this juncture we must again emphasize this particular interaction between morality as a persuasion and morality as the sumtotal of deeds. To start with the perspective of the status of individuals, which means starting with the perspective of individuality, would be impossible, unless we are guided by and grounded in an interpretation of the human situation. This is a rather strong and narrow interpretation because it separates individuals from the factual contexts and concurrently projects on them the perspective of being human, i.e. a universal perspective, universal in that it connotes human features and qualities not confined to any context or to any sentiments arising between individuals. It is not because we encounter somebody as our neighbour or happen to love him or have any passionate attachment to him that we recognize him as an individual and that we expect his recognition of ourselves as individuals, thus attempting to create modes of recognition and codes of behaviour based on it. An individual in any factual encounter has specific needs, and the very factual context emphasizes these and provides for means of satisfying them. The moral perspective, while isolating the individuals, looks at them outside their needs, that is to say, from the inside of their locus or position as individuals in the abstract ontological sense of the term. But here we immediately come across the dialectic of the moral perspective, once it is translated into a moral activity. Recognition of the individual as such has to find expression in responding to the individual as he really or factually is, that is to say, in responding to his needs, which are always of a factual character. Hence the question arises: what is new about the moral dimension, once it becomes the well-spring of the moral action and thus is mediated by the factual encounter and recognizes the imperative of taking factual needs into account by recognizing them and acting accordingly. It seems to be the case that from this point of view morality becomes the question of conviction or disposition, of what Kant called *die Gesinnung*. We can take care of the individual in his factual needs for help or medical care, housing or education, within the primary human context, in that we are motivated by the sense of belonging, by philanthropy, by being passionately interested in doing something where passion is manifested in doing *qua* helping. In this context moral activity, amounting to *Gesinnung* and motivated by it, connotes an activity based on the recognition of the individual as such outside his ties of co-existence and, from the point of view of the doer, above this involvement in the factual situation, that is to say, as motivated by the abstract notion of recognition which implies both the recognition of the individual and his universal position. Such an activity, rooted in a perspective which becomes a *Gesinnung*, is therefore much more interpretative than activities which take advantage of given situations or of given needs, such as the need to survive or to exchange goods, or even to find leisure and recreation. Moral activity appears therefore from this point of view as an activity based on a philosophical interpretation of the world, more so than in the case of the activities which we have already discussed. Therefore the question arises: how and to what extent does that interpretation lead to the recognition of individuals and to mutuality of recognition among them, founded on a factual ground, or is it perhaps a mere invention and as such resembling play? We now turn to this issue.

(2)

If we may use in the context the common distinction between 'inside' and 'outside', it can be said that from the outside, i.e. from the point of view of the observer or the surroundings, no individual is an integrated entity. Hence in this case we cannot even apply the notion of individual, the 'I', the 'ego', etc. What is tangible from the outside are acts, deeds, interventions, even when we distinguish, as we do, between what occurs involuntarily — like the circulation of the blood — and voluntarily — like taking a walk —, though obviously that distinction implies the concept of the agent who performs the voluntary act. But the acts as such in their visible shape and occurrence do not immediately imply, or certainly do not indicate, an agent or an individual, the 'I', etc. This is so since the individual as the 'I' is a concept through which the individual defines himself. The 'I' is essentially a circular or self-reflective notion. Through and in that notion, while denoting oneself, one attributes to oneself certain deeds which in turn are recognizable from the outside. The observer from the outside may attribute the deeds to an 'I', but only on the assumption that there is an 'I' and therefore a self-reflective entity attributing to himself certain deeds and making himself into an 'I' or an individual in and by those acts of attribution. There is no beginning to the 'I', and this is only the reverse of the previous description of the circularity of the 'I'. The 'I', and this certainly applies to the notion of the individual, is both an act and an entity. The act of attribution or denoting is in itself a fragmented act, and it is so even when it is not visible as the act of voting or raising one's hand. But the sporadic act connects one act of attribution to another, and thus creates a chain. That chain in turn is interpreted not only as a chain in time but as an entity expressing itself in time and attributing to itself distinct acts in time. Thus self-attributing has both an instantaneous meaning and a permanent one, and therefore the individual or the 'I' occupies two levels simultaneously: the level of acts and the level of integration of acts into a constant entity. There is, to put it differently, an act of attributing to oneself and an act of affirming oneself as oneself. Memory would not be possible or would lack its support were it not for this act of typing up an occurrence and its traces with other occurences. Memory is to some extent the operative or the functional manifestation of the constancy of the ego, in spite of the fact that the ego does not exist but for the sum-total of his recollections. There emerges a profound question: 'how do I know that the 'I' of this moment is the 'I' of yesterday?' The answer to this question is that it is the 'I' himself who establishes the constancy of the moments and that he is the same 'I' because he knows that he is the same 'I'. Again the aspect of knowledge and the aspect of being are interrelated. We cannot here accept the Cartesian view starting only with the *cogito* and moving to the *sum*, because the *cogito* acknowledges the *sum*, and the awareness of the constancy of the *sum* reinforces the self-denoting and the self-attributing. Since we cannot start with one pole only, we would rather refer to the position of the individual or of the 'I' as being grounded in, and expressive of, what might be described as a continuous chain of integrating acts. The integration in this case refers to attribution of deeds and feelings, but also to the attribution of the ego to itself. Here, too, we cannot distinguish between activity and entity; the two aspects mutually reinforce each other.

The question of the mutual recognition or even acknowledgement between different individuals cannot be — and this goes without saying — detached from this circular character of attribution and the continuous self-establishment of the individual or the 'I'. The traditional attempts to indicate one attitude that can explain the interpretation of an entity as an *alter ego* are basically wrong, because these attempts try to identify one mode of cognition and recognition explaining and warranting the assessment and affirmation of the presence of the *alter ego*. But, as a matter of fact, the ego as such is not encountered, let alone the *alter ego*. The ego is established by itself continuously, and therefore the encounter between individuals presupposes the notion of attribution; it is an extension of the notion of an attribution from oneself to the *alter ego*. Hence it has indeed the element of analogy as well as that of empathy which is stressed in the traditional analyses of the perplexing situation between the 'I' and 'Thou'. But the direct acts would not be possible without the notion of self-attribution and without broadening the scope of self-reflection, which one experiences and presupposes within his own orbit and, by the same token, presupposes as being attributable to the other — the very attribution creating or affirming the other as an entity. It thus creates or affirms the other within my own horizon on the assumption that the other is an 'I' in his own orbit. At this point we may agree to a statement by Fichte in *Das System der Sittenlehre*, though we must somehow try to mitigate it: 'What actually (*eigentlich*) am I, that is to say what kind of an individual am I? And what is the ground (*Grund*) that I am this? I answer: I am from the moment at which I came to consciousness, the one into whom I am making myself with freedom, and I am this because I am making myself to this.'[1] We must take exception to what can be described as Fichte's leap to the concept of freedom, though it may be important for the establishment of the concept and is thus essential from the angle of the moral activity. We describe the activity to which Fichte refers without immediately charging it with the connotation, let alone the moral implications, of freedom. What is significant is to emphasize the self-assertive position of the individual or of the 'I'. Therefore the 'I' is both a fact and a construction or, to put it paradoxically, a non-factual fact.

The question which now arises is: what is the significance or bearing of the analysis of the position of the individual or the 'I' from the point of view of moral activity, and to what extent does that analysis contribute to the understanding of moral activity and to the description of its inherent problematic situation? There are several aspects which must be considered from this point of departure, in order to attempt an elucidation of the nature of moral activity.

(3)

In the first place we are bound to recognize that the concept of the moral agent as the doer or as the subject related to and nevertheless detached from the act presupposes the notion of the

1. *Das System der Sittenlehre nach den Prinzipien der Wissenschaftslehre*, included in Fichte's *Werke*, zw. Bd., ed. Medicus, Meiner, Leipzig, (n.d.) p. 226.

'I'. Fichte, as we have seen in the quotation, by introducing the concept or freedom, immediately gave the 'I' a moral connotation or even identified the self-affirmative character of the 'I' with freedom, assuming, or implying, that freedom has an immediate moral nuance because it points to spontaneity, to lack of constraint, to the open spaces, etc. We cannot follow this line because we must take freedom, being the presupposition for decisions, as only one of the explications of the self-affirmation of the 'I'. The 'I', by attributing acts, deeds, sentiments to himself, can turn himself into a decision-maker and become a moral agent. Self-direction is an extension of attribution and affirmation, but the two are not identical. It is because of this difference between the, as it were, neutral self-affirmation and the focused affirmation *qua* decision that we must presuppose the position of the 'I', in order to ground in it the position of the moral agent, insofar as the moral agent is a deciding agent.

This consideration will become even more salient when we consider the relationship between self-affirmation and self-responsibility. To be responsible connotes, at least in part, the attribution of deeds and their consequences to an agent, attribution by one's fellow-man or by society or by oneself. Self-attribution in the pre-moral sense is therefore the presupposition of attribution in the sense of responsibility, implying that one carries the onus or the accountability for one's deeds. Hence the minimal presupposition for being responsible is to be an agent. Moreover, to be a responsible agent is to be a constant agent, since we cannot attribute deeds only to deeds (in the causal sense this is possible, but in the sense prescribed by the notion of responsibility it is not). Hence the self-affirmation in the continuous sense of that notion is again a minimal presupposition for carrying the burden of responsibility. In this sense self-affirmation is a more basic notion than the notion of responsibility and the first is a *conditio sine qua non* for the second. Broadening this consideration we may say that the reference to the precondition for the notion and the position of the agent — and therefore necessarily of the moral agent — is the reference to the 'I' or to the individual. At this point we come to the following issue, whether there can be a moral activity without implying a moral agent, or in other words, whether at the threshold of the moral activity we cease to be concerned only with acts and deeds and reach the level of an agent who is engaged in activities but who is more than the mere scattered activities. We have seen in our previous analysis, mainly in the analysis of work and labour, that the presence of the agent is somehow superimposed on the activities of labour and the exchangeability of goods. When reaching the point of moral activity we arrive at the level where the notion of the agent emerges not only in order to round up the sphere of activity but in order to explicate the very meaning of the sphere of moral activity. This is so because of the emergence of the aspect of justification concurrently with the aspect of the agent. That aspect will be our next concern.

(4)

As a matter of fact, moral activity presupposes its being preceded by the moral perspective, and its justification invests it with a perspective that is a presupposition for action. Justification implies — and this is obvious — a position of legitimacy. The moral perspective leads to the assertion of the position which the agent occupies. The agent expresses himself in the first place, again in a circular way, in his claim to be an agent, or in his demand to be acknowledged as an agent. Here, too, to be an agent in one's own eyes, and to be an agent in the inter-personal context are two sides of the same coin. One recognizes oneself as an agent, one may demand of oneself to be such, in the sense of living up to one's own expectations e.g. to be responsible, stable, consistent, more than a sum-total of erratic deeds, and one demands from another agent the recognition of one's position. Here mutuality becomes apparent. A demand is directed toward oneself, and concurrently to another agent; that aspect of the demand for recognition is in turn the meaning of the moral perspective. Insofar as to be an agent is to be justifiably so, the moral perspective reinforces not only the position of the agent but also his right to be an agent — and here the ontological status of the agent and the moral affirmation of that status overlap, or mutually reinforce each other.

The reinforcement of the position of the agent by the moral perspective becomes important in more specific attitudes or responses which in turn lead us from the moral perspective to the moral act. One of the most significant expressions of the moral reinforcement of being an agent is the legitimacy of the demand for freedom of thought and, following it, freedom of expression, assuming a line of continuity from thought to expression. Freedom of thought is essential or basic in the context in view of the relationship pertaining between being and thinking. Since thinking is essential for being an ego, the moral perspective lends its approval to the position of the ego as an agent by granting legitimacy to his right to think. Thus the emphasis is placed on the activity of thinking and not on the thoughts entertained in that activity. But since there is no thinking without thoughts, even in the vaguest sense of the term, the legitimacy of thinking bestows the aspect of legitimacy on thoughts, and, following this, on the expression of thoughts. Here, too, the component of reciprocity or mutuality is central because the legitimacy applies not only to one's own ego but to ego in general or to egos in the plural. Therefore legitimacy leads to reciprocity in terms of the context of the agents and eventually their mutuality.

Following this line we can discern attitudes related to the position of the ego which carry a moral significance, such as, for instance, the attitude of encouraging a person. To encourage is to create an atmosphere germane to the maintenance of the position of the agent and to the expression of his potentialities. Encouragement in turn may take more concrete shapes, such as encouragement of one's abilities, encouragement of one's expressions, self-confidence, etc. The legitimacy of the attitude of encouragement is grounded in the addressee of the encouragement, the agent or the person. The understanding is that the agent can exist as an agent only when he is active or when he operates. Therefore, like the acknowledgement of the right to thoughts and expressions, the acknowledgement of the right or the demand to be encouraged are different attitudes aimed simultaneously at the maintenance and the activization of the agent, on the presupposition that were it not for such activization, the agent would cease to be an agent. An opaque agent is a contradiction in terms.

Some moral dilemmas are again related to that basic position of the agent. A most momentous problem, which has become central in present-day behaviour and discussion (mainly in what goes by the name: medical ethics), is to what extent the maintenance of the body is the maintenance of the agent. In other words, whether or not the encouragement can be reduced to the most basic level of existence from the biological aspect, or whether it basically implies the total agents as its addressee, including the physical aspect of his existence, but by no means that aspect alone.

At this juncture we notice a singular coalescence of the reflective perspective of the 'I' and the moral perspective of the agent, and concomitant, more concrete, attitudes like encouragement, etc. Perhaps one could pose the following question: do the moral perspective and the activity which follows it appear as a response to a need, as an elaboration of a fact, or are they something *sui generis* and as such are to be lodged outside any factual description, including the driving forces grounded in needs. Let us recall at this point the previous analysis of work as being grounded in the need of the organism to subsist, and the analysis of political activity which appears as a continuous re-creation of coexistence with the proviso that the very fact of coexistence is never initiated *ex nihilo*. We do not find parallel roots for moral activity since, as we have seen, the agent is not a fact but a continuous creation, since the 'I' is not a fact but a continuous activity reinterpreting himself and keeping on creating himself via that re-creation. We wonder, therefore, what is the basic need to which we can refer in order to define the relationship between the activity and the need to be served or satisfied by the activity. It could be said that, since we relate the moral perspective and moral activity to the position of the 'I', we are by definition unable to identify a need. The 'I' is a total entity while a need is a partial driving force, an awareness of something lacking, and as such, in a way, presupposes the 'I' who, being aware, turns the changes in the circulation of the blood, for instance, into felt needs. If there is a need in the context, it is a need to reinforce the very position of the 'I' or, put differently, the moral interpretation of the 'I' as an agent is a reinforcement of the ego as a reflective entity. The acknowledgement or the very aspect of acknowledgement, which is of course present within the orbit of the individual 'I' but becomes more visible and tangible within the inter-human context, is therefore the validation of the

'I' as an entity. The 'I' demands to be recognized as such; that demand becomes palpable in the inter-human context, and the mutual recognition or acknowledgement appear as justification for the existence of the 'I'. In this sense the moral perspective serves, if anything, the need of the 'I' to be an 'I'. Put differently – the acknowledgement contributes to self-knowledge. It is in this sense that we can interpret the saying that the greatest need is to be needed, that is to say, that the essential need is to be understood as an 'I' in one's own eyes and in the inter-personal realm.

We do not intend to say that without the moral perspective and the modes of acknowledgement which follow it and become seeds of moral activity the 'I' would not exist. Neither do we intend to say that the shift from the 'I' to the agent is a shift which pre-supposes or calls for the moral perspective. We intend to say that the moral perspective reinforces the position of the 'I' by making the very assertion into a demand, though we are not oblivious of the fact that a demand is weaker than a reality since a demand lacks the compelling character of reality. Acknowledgement is always a reflective attitude, unlike the impact of an im-posed reality which has to be taken simply as a fact and whose legitimacy need not be acknowledged. An imposition is strong enough even when it is not legitimate, while legitimacy as a per-spective is to some extent a compensation for the lack of an immediate impact, since an immediate impact is by definition im-possible within the realm of acknowledged demands. Amplifying this point we can say: since the human being is basically a weak entity, not only physically or because of his finitude, the integrity of his position is never safeguarded. It is never ostensibly visible; hence the moral perspective is some sort of help extended to the weak and vulnerable human being. That help appears over and above any services rendered to the human being, in the very attitude of recognition and acknowledgement and in the very mutuality pertaining or that should pertain between individual human beings.

We may here distinguish between coexistence and mutuality. We have seen that coexistence calls for a continuous interpretation of the components of coexistence. Basically coexistence refers to an embracing framework, to a common space shared, or to a common lineage whose descendants we are. Coexistence does not imply the mutuality between individual human beings and their reciprocal acknowledgement. The innovation of the moral perspective is that as such it does not create a community as a common space, but continually endeavours to create the common ground out of the sources or origins of mutual acknowledgement. Acknowledgement precedes community; here again the moral perspective and the activity which follows it seem to have more of an abstract character than the activities analyzed before, because the recogniton of mutuality grounded in reciprocal acknowledgement is more abstract than, e.g., the recognition of a common lineage or exchange of commodities.

A comment on one of the formulations of Kant's categorical imperative is not out of place at this juncture: 'Act in such a way that you always treat humanity, whether in your own person or in the person of any other, never simply as a means, but always at the same time as an end.'[2] Let us distinguish, in terms of this formulation, between its first part, which refers to humanity in the person, and its second part, which refers to the distinction between means and ends. In Kant's system and formulations they are indeed closely connected. Yet it seems that we can distinguish between them by identifying the respective arguments behind them. The reference to humanity is an attempt to interpret the person, the 'I' or the agent, as a manifestation of the common essence which is humanity or humaneness. Every person, being a manifestation, presupposes the common ground. Therefore one's respect towards a person is respect towards the common ground, manifesting itself in a diffuse way among the variety of persons coexisting now and dispersed throughout the generations of the past and of the future. We know from Kant's philosophy of history that it is imperative to take future generations into account, because they are manifestations of the human common ground. In this sense Kant thought that the moral perspective and the moral deeds, implied in following the categorical imperative, presuppose a metaphysical entity of humanity which as such transcends the

2. Immanuel Kant: *Groundwork of the Metaphysics and Morals*, translated and analyzed by H.J. Paton, Harper Torchbooks/The Academy Library, Harper & Row, New York and Evanston, 1964, p. 96.

the orbit of the 'I' or of the agent. Strange as it may sound — and this is a criticism of Kant's view — according to Kant moral activity did not rely only on moral perspective and on the grounding of that perspective in the position of the 'I'. He looked for a 'supra-facticity', namely humanity, to give the mutual acknowledgement characteristic of the moral perspective and expressing itself in moral activity, not a circular but a linear character, i.e. to ground it in humanity. Since reciprocity must create the community out of its own resources, Kant attempted to circumvent the indefinite character of that community — such a community is never present and can never be delineated — and transformed it from its position as the final aim of moral activity into its presupposed ground. The agents do not create, or do not only create, humanity; humanity is presupposed. To be sure, in this sense, Kant's theory is an attempt to ground morality not in a need but still in a fact, though not a tangible one. We shall now consider the second part of the formulation of the categorical imperative.

(5)

As we have seen, Kant replaces the reciprocity of the relationship between persons by the common essence, or at least he attempts to establish the ground of that reciprocity in the common essence. His reasoning seems to be the following: it is more warranted or plausible to consider a person as an end when the considering person and the considered share the same essence, than if that consideration were only a decision or were encompassed merely by the context of reciprocity. What indeed is the meaning of treating a person as an end, and not just as a means? Kant usually refers to the attitude of respect (*Achtung*) without fully elaborating the meaning of this attitude or at least its nuances. It must in the first place be said that to be an end is a position, namely an ultimate state or status. As opposed to being a means it signifies an ultimate position and not an instrument. There is always a possibility of treating a person as a means, that is to say, as one yielding some benefit. That attitude is present even on the level of exchangeability, where I am rewarded by the service rendered or by the goods exchanged. There can be 'an honest exchangeability' which is still related, however, to rewards or benefits. Kant aimed at separating the moral attitude from the attitude of the expected reward, and therefore he referred to the position of being an end. An end calls for deference, and deference may in turn call for active approaches like looking after or taking care of somebody, those approaches transcending the attitudinal aspect of holding him in esteem, and even more so of taking notice of him. Negatively expressed, the attitude of holding in respect has the consequence of refraining from causing injury. In Kant's eyes to regard somebody only as a means already causes him injury, at least in the sense that regarding somebody as a means only places him in a position where he is constantly and continuously at the disposal of the other, and therefore is both reflectively and practically exploited. If this interpretation is correct, then we reach the conclusion that to be an end is to be involved in a context of mutual regard expressed in equal esteem, that is to say, that nobody is to be placed in the position of being at the disposal of another; at least, being at another's disposal has to be mitigated and perhaps remedied by being an end, that is to say, by occupying an independent position *vis-à-vis* the other. Hence we come back to the aspect of reciprocity in evaluation which is projected in terms of the common essence or, if not projected, is held as a self-supporting position, initiating a moral attitude without the need to regress to the common essence *qua* humanity as the human race.

From this point we may take an additional step in our attempt to describe the position of morality both as a perspective and as an activity. This may be formulated in the following way: morality as a perspective applies not only to moral activity in the limited sense of the term, namely, to the attitude of mutual acknowledgement, respect, etc. It applies also to other activities, for instance, to the activity of exchanging goods or playing and to political activities in their historical manifestations and processes. In the area of work or economic activity, a kind of mutuality is present in the exchange, in the mutual reliance, in the contract made or in the presupposition that one's own deed will be remunerated by the deed of another person or the goods produced by him. Economic activity or work do not have to regress to the intentions of the acts performed and to the internalization which takes place, because the need as such is the driving force and the mutuality itself in this case is self-supporting. The moral consideration, i.e. moral perspective and its consequences in moral behaviour, bring into the activity, which has its own structure and propensity, the intention — for instance to exchange goods in order to manifest human reciprocity or, eventually, in practice and more concretely — concern, care, etc. The aspect of intentions becomes paramount in two senses, namely, whether or not we behave in an honest way, that is to say, being guided by standards and not only having in mind the benefit which will accrue to the agent; and in the second sense that we turn the sphere of exchangeability into one of a manifestation of human reciprocity, mutual respect and care which perhaps, on an abstract level, appear as 'purely' moral but on the concrete level appear as involved or manifest in concrete acts of taking care, providing goods, food, etc. Here indeed the political sphere becomes prominent, since organized society provides services for human beings, giving momentum to production and consumption, relying, to some extent, on forces of exchangeability but attempting to base them upon human mutuality and direct them by human inter-personal acknowledgement, esteem and care. In this sense moral perspective and its concomitant activity turn out to be a kind of meta-activity, penetrating or percolating through activities of different sorts, bringing into prominence the aspect of intentions or the aspect of mutuality as such. Precisely because the moral perspective and the moral activity are more abstract than the activities of exchangeability and politics, they can apply to the former, the abstract being, as it were, broader and more flexible than the concrete. In addition, because of the emphasis placed on intentions, there is no need and no point in changing the given structure or the *raison d'être* of the concrete activities by investing them with a moral meaning. Here again the notion of moral 'perspective' is significant, because morality transcends mere activity, being also a point of view or an attitude. As such it can be applied to activities which have their momentum in themselves but can be reinforced or even directed, because of the motivation stemming from the moral perspective.

(6)

Moral perspective, therefore, reinforces the activities on their own level. But just the same, we should see the other side of the coin. The emphasis placed on intentions, that emphasis which in a sense makes the moral activity flexible and applicable, can also make it rigid and perhaps even cruel — in the sense of *fiat iustitia pereat mundus*. Our regard for the human being may lead to an interpretation which can be put in the following way: a human being is regarded as a moral agent; as a moral agent he is by definition active; therefore he must take care of himself; therefore he should be self-sufficient. Our respect for him depends upon his respect for us, etc. Because of this circularity we may easily remain immersed in attitudes, in intentions, in evaluations and may miss the breakthrough to concrete acts; we may make these concrete acts totally dependent upon their origins in the intentions out of which they ought to flow. This is sometimes a cruelty with good intentions, but a cruelty pertaining to an attitude which remains in self-enclosed abstractness, due to the moral perspective which does not find flexibility for its own application in concrete situations and via the concrete needs of human beings. In this sense the meta-character of moral perspective and moral activity is both an advantage and a disadvantage. It is an advantage because it can apply the moral approach to different spheres of inter-human relations, between men and women, between grown-ups and children, between partners, etc. The moral attitude can be maintained despite the variegation of the different spheres to be guided by the moral concern. The disadvantage lies in the lack of translation of acknowledgement, reciprocity, esteem, into day-to-day deeds, precisely because of this tendency to make the moral sphere self-supportive and thus in a way turn morality into over-morality or excessive morality. This propensity towards 'over-doing' is characteristic of structures of actions in general, when for instance exchangeability becomes an exclusive norm, or political considerations for bringing about coexistence and reinforcing it become the exclusive considerations. In a way the same 'exaggerated logic' applies to the moral sphere as well, though that sphere, out of its own resources, calls for an application in concrete situations and should therefore be regarded as being open in the first place, or, at least, as being capable of being so. Moral perspective is certainly capable of being open, and is — as we shall see — essentially so, but that capability is not automatically translated into concrete openness.

Directing our attention to this possible rigidity of the moral sphere leads us to an additional consideration of the relationship pertaining between the moral sphere and reality as such, reality in terms both of the surrounding world and of inter-human contexts. We have already seen that morality is related to a continuous self-interpretation of human beings who consider themselves as agents, giving a different connotation to that term and that position. Morality introduces a perspective, but does not create a reality. Within the given reality of the plurality of human beings it introduces the aspect of the position of being an agent concurrently with the attitude of mutual acknowledgement *qua* agents. The limitation of the moral activity lies precisely in its interpretative character. From this point of view an additional conclusion has to emerge: moral perspective is a total perspective since it refers to the total position of man being an agent. But the realization of that perspective through concrete deeds is a piecemeal realization here and now, and thus is also related to the particular circumstances. The relatedness to the circumstances is positively prescribed by taking seriously the concrete situations in which human beings find themselves, but also by taking seriously the abstract position of the agent who, by virtue of his existence, is removed from that abstractness. He finds himself in concrete situations and interprets himself — and is interpreted also by his fellow-men — as an agent implicated in situations; equal emphasis has to be given to both aspects of the human situation. The mistake of the relativistic interpretation lies in its disregarding the total perspective, and the absolutistic rigidity of morality lies in its disregarding any involvement in concrete conditions which in a sense may be accidental. But in another sense it brings into prominence the systematic position of morality: it does not create a reality but intervenes in it and evaluates it according to the standard established by viewing the person as an agent involved in the inter-human context of reciprocal acknowledgement. Here again it has to be observed that Kant's interpretation of morality with its emphasis on intentions *qua Gesinnung*, warranted as it is, does not do full justice to the interrelation between the empirical and the trans-empirical aspects of morality. Kant, as is well known, emphasized only the trans-empirical aspect of morality, and thus, accordingly, over-emphasized it.

(7)

At this juncture an exploration of the concept of freedom and its bearing upon moral activity and moral perspective is structurally or phenomenologically justified. Let us start with a delineation of the boundaries of the concept of freedom, suggesting some preliminary distinctions and definitions. Negatively speaking, freedom implies or connotes independence from compulsion, once compulsion connotes an external imposition on the action or on the agent. In this sense freedom implies a separation from an overriding determination; moreover, a separation due to the actions of the separated being. There is no given, permanent, or constant separation. An act is implied which separates itself from the imposed determination and thus separates the agent and constitutes him. This separation amounts to what is traditionally called negative freedom. But there is no separation unless there is an act giving rise to this separation. Therefore to some extent the act of separation is an expression of positive freedom or at least a precondition for positive freedom, once we add to the separation a new determination or a determination starting that act. By definition an act has a content or a meaning, and thus gives direction. In this sense freedom implies some aspect of determination as opposed to the broad system of determination imposed on acts or on agents. Since freedom implies a direction, either immediately or at least as a precondition for its direction, it opens up a vista for questions about the meaning or the significance of that direction. We therefore ask the question: 'what has been acted upon?' and we combine two evaluations: (a) the evaluation of the act itself and (b) the evaluation of the content or direction of the act.

Moral perspective implies the evaluation of the very position of freedom as self-determination. Yet, as we see, that position is coterminous with an act or an activity; therefore we cannot separate the moral perspective from the moral act. The justification of the act lies in its very self-creation which leads to a further justification in terms of the outcome of the self-determination, its result, or perhaps its intention. In this sense freedom creates itself, and we can subscribe to a random statement by Kant, 'we must be free in order to be able to make purposive use of our powers in freedom.'[3] This circular character of freedom, which amounts to self-separation from the chain of determination or the establishment of self-determination, is parallel to the circular character of the position of the 'I' with which we started the present part of our discussion. As the 'I' creates himself continuously, so self-determination continuously creates and reinforces itself by its very separation from the determining chain of events. Moreover, there is an additional parallelism between the 'I' and the notion of freedom. The 'I' is a total entity, though never present as such, because present are only scattered acts of perception, conception, awareness, cognition, decision, etc. The 'I' is a self-totalization of these acts insofar as acts are viewed as manifestations of the 'I', though the 'I' in turn is viewed as a progressing totalization of the acts, a totalization which never reaches consummation. Similarly, there are acts of detachment from the surrounding chains; their totalization is considered to be freedom, though factually there are only scattered, indeed to some extent continuous, acts which are free according to the definition of self-determination. Because of this totalization, which is present on the level of both cognitive and of determining, that is self-determining, acts towards action, it can be said that freedom is coterminous with being an agent, or that freedom is an attribute of an agent. An agent who is directed towards action and not only towards conception is a free agent. To be free is therefore on the one hand a self-interpretation of the 'I' and on the other his self-determination; here we observe the shift from interpretation to determination, the latter implying direction to-

---

3. Immanuel Kant: *Religion within the Limits of Reason Alone*, translated with an introduction and notes by Theodore M. Greene and Hoyt H. Hudson, with an essay by John R. Silber, Harper Torchbooks/The Cloister Library, Harper & Row, New York and Evanston, 1960, p. 176, Note.

wards action and not only direction towards self-reflection. The moral perspective brings about a double evaluation: the agent, affirming himself as an agent, affirms that which is good in the first place, because to be a self-determining agent (and this is perhaps a pleonastic expression, since to be an agent is to be self-determining) is good in itself; by the same token it is a precondition for actions which in turn can be evaluated according as to whether or not they serve objectives or ends which are good and must be viewed as such. Freedom in the total sense implies or realizes a norm which we may call a positional norm, whereas freedom as giving momentum to action calls for an evaluation not from the positional point of view but from what might be called a thematic point of view according to what we have acted upon, what direction our action takes, etc.

The two aspects of freedom converge to some extent when we understand freedom not only as a totalization of acts and the presupposed capacity to act, but also as acting in the direction of opening oneself to one's fellow-man, to his needs, to one's respect for him, etc. Why is freedom implied in this direction or in that attitude? It is implied because — again — the interpretative character of our approach to our fellow-man and to reciprocity itself implies interpretation of the datum encountered as the fellow-man. The fellow-man is not just opaquely given; he is conceived as man, as fellow-man, and this very conception presupposes our openness towards him. To put it negatively, we are not determined by the mere data but approach them from our vantage point and recognize them not only in their simple givenness but in their significance or meaning. To view a datum as a person or as an agent is to be open towards it or in a sense to accept it as another 'I' or as an agent in the framework of our encounter interpreted in the context of reciprocity. This affirmation of the fellow-man and the concomitant attitude is one of openness. Here openness runs counter to the position of being pre-determined — and thus closed — by the chain of deterministically conducted events or emerging situations. But again openness is not only an attitude but is also a morally evaluated position, since it is either implied in reciprocity or viewed as a precondition for reciprocity. We thus can say that the primary position of freedom in the moral sphere is due to its proximity to the 'I'. It is also a minimal interpretation of the 'I' in moral term concurrently with a maximal interpretation. To be free is already a moral position. But this is a moral position grounded in the position of the 'I'. It is a moral position from the thematic aspect, because only freedom can lead to openness and thereby to the various modes of the underlying reciprocity.

We can elaborate on the aspect of freedom by referring to its relation to the aspect of intention, which we identified as having a basic moral significance. Sometimes we say about freedom that it refers not only to an act performed but to an act chosen or willed. Obviously the element of choice or will refers to the intentional character of the action or to the internal aspect of a deed. Yet the suggested interpretation of freedom prohibits its identification with choice, and particularly with will, which at most is one of many manifestations or attributes of the 'I' or the agent. To be an 'I' is a situation of freedom, certainly so when the 'I' posits himself in the horizon of actions and their directions. Thus it would be at the most a *pars pro toto* interpretation to assume one aspect of freedom, for instance will, and to identify freedom with will or to refer to the primary synthesis which is called freedom of will. In one sense will is interpreted as a carrier of freedom because freedom is presupposed in the first place, and we are looking for a partial carrier of the total agent. But there can be nothing in the part that is not present in the total. Therefore the intentional character of freedom has to be understood in its relation to the position of the 'I' and not to the position of the will. At this point, strange as it may sound, even Kant's system of morality is obscured by an ambiguity, since Kant relates freedom either to reason or to the will or to both. It is systematically more plausible to present a primary totality or synthesis instead of looking for a *post factum* synthesis like that between reason and will. We shall now see the consequences of the position of freedom on the borderline between reflection and activity in regard to the moral sphere in the more limited sense of the term. We therefore come back to the consideration of human reciprocity.

(8)

Within the context of reciprocity freedom as openness connotes the recognition of the other person's freedom or, in short, that the other person is a free person. Therefore, he is open to his fellow-men, as is the person with whom we started in our description and exploration. In the context of mutuality we thus find a combination of the basic recognition with certain modes expressing that recognition, such as mutual concern, response, care, help, etc. In the moral sphere reciprocity is guided by two considerations: (a) on the basic level the consideration for freedom and its mutual acknowledgement; and (b) on the empirical level the consideration for the position of the free human being, in which he is placed empirically, and which in turn has to be viewed from two perspectives: his empirical position is part of his position as a free agent and therefore calls for recognition, affirmation, and the various manifestations of heed and care. But the empirical position is also one of instrumental significance for the free agent, that is to say, if he is not taken care of empirically, his position of freedom might be meaningless. Hence in the moral situation we find a double intentionality: one towards the empirical position in its diversity, the other towards the basic position which upholds the empirical position and in turn is maintained by it.

At this point we again realize the meta-character of the moral consideration as one permeating activities of a different sort, for instance the activity of labour leading towards exchangeability. From the moral point of view we interpret exchangeability as mutuality. We add the perspective of maintaining the mutuality as such, and not only the mutuality as exchangeability limiting itself to the mutual benefit of the partners. To play on the words we may say: while exchangeability in its own limited sphere applies the principle *do ut des*, moral perspective introduces the principle of *do et des*. But in addition, within the context of mutuality and in spite of it, moral perspective may lead to the imperative, which eventually amounts to renouncing or at least deferring mutuality — just *do* without *des*, when we are concerned with the position of our fellow-man, perhaps with his inaptitude to be factually engaged in mutuality, either because of his physical or mental incapacity or because we project mutuality beyond the present encounter, as we do, for instance, with children. Yet, when we totally disregard the aspect of mutuality — paradoxical as this may sound — and engage in care or concern as expressing our own attitude, we may disregard the actual or potential position of our fellow-man, and thus perhaps be philanthropic but not necessarily moral in the proper sense, once morality is grounded in the notion of mutual acknowledgement and expectations based on that mutuality. Moreover, in a moral situation, we find ourselves continuously facing the dilemma of striking an equilibrium between the positional acknowledgement of the other person as a free man, and the empirical attitudes and deeds meant to express that acknowledgement and to establish it empirically. A philanthropic attitude is guided, at least to some extent, by the empirical encounter and leaves aside the positional horizon of freedom and thus that of mutuality. Yet the emphasis on freedom only may be empty, if we make no attempt to apply the principle of mutuality or at least the recognition of freedom to the context as it exists here and now and not as it is created by the free agent. On the contrary, the free agent is free in spite of his empirical condition, and we recognize that duality pertaining to him; in the moral sphere we are called to act according to the empirical description of the situation, attributing the situation to the free agent and conceiving the situation not as an extension of the freedom but as a condition *malgré* freedom. Thus, out of moral considerations, we are led to various attempts at bringing together an activity like the striving towards material subsistence with the moral perspective of freedom. This conjunction of considerations leads us to the conclusion that without means at the level of subsistence there will be no free agent, but the free agent must maintain his freedom beyond the empirical situations in which he is involved. Granting or presupposing openness here implies both a separation of the free agent from the empirical mode of his existence, e.g. subsistence and its problems, and his involvement in that situation. At this point the moral perspective, while leading to a particular attitude, is guided by a certain interpretation of the data, by placing the data on different levels and then reverting to attitudes and imperatives guided by interpretation on the one hand and enhancing the interpretation on the other.

(9)

At this point it does not seem too late to ask the rather trivial question: where does the notion or attribute of good or goodness come into the moral sphere, or, to take advantage of the distinctions already presented, where does it come in from the point of view of the moral perspective and the activity grounded in it?

Let us start, perhaps more didactically than systematically, by introducing an intermediate concept, that of benevolence, in St. Thomas' sense of *benignitas* which is also present in the German expression *Gütigkeit*. If we translate *benignitas*, at least following its root, as a benign attitude, it can be said that this attitude amounts to openness in its different expressions, or to openness even when we do not attempt, as we did in our preceding exploration, to ground it in freedom. Openness, as a benign attitude, is to be understood as the attitude of granting, serving, understanding, caring, etc. But not only in the day-to-day vernacular do we understand goodness as a benign attitude or as openness, as an attitude leading to giving, but this basic meaning is maintained also in systematic philosophical interpretations. It is maintained to some extent in Plato's idea of the good and the parable of the sun, since the idea of the good makes the good, like the sun, visible, as it also makes the eyes see them both. Thus goodness implies granting certain features to, and bringing together, the poles of the 'I' and the thing. Let us also mention a further example from the history of philosophical ideas, namely Leibnitz's question; why does something exist rather than nothing? This question asks for the reason why something exists, and exists thus and not otherwise, and, as is well known, Leibnitz ultimately has recourse to the notion of God, saying that the ultimate reason of things is God. But God is not only an ultimate reason as a necessary being lying outside the sequence of contingent things, but also because in the essence of God, according to the interpretation epitomized by Leibnitz, as a perfect being is to posit things and thus grant them existence; and our emphasis would here be both on granting in general and on granting existence in particular.[4] Hence we can understand the philosophical interpretations of the attribute or essence of granting as amplifying the notion of *benignitas* by extending them beyond the inter-human context and situating them as the ultimate ground of reality. To go one step further it can be said that the quality or the attribute of goodness comes into the context of morality because it can be related to the positional character of freedom as the ultimate ground of openness and as the ultimate ground of decisions and deeds. It expresses openness from the point of view of the agent as well as from the point of view of the recipient of the deeds and the addressee of the attitudes. Yet this is only one side of our attempt to present a sort of mitigated 'deduction' of the concept of the good or goodness in its inherent presence in the moral sphere — and we deliberately started, as indicated before, from a very partial construction. Hence it is essential to take the second step, which leads to a more significant aspect than the first.

(10)

The question of the intrinsic relationship between the notion of the good and the notion and position of freedom calls for an exploration or again for a kind of 'deduction'. At this point we suggest that the aspect of the good in its thematic connotation and the aspect of 'ought', which can be viewed as the positional description of the good or goodness, are intertwined. With this comment as preface let us ask what makes freedom a good or good. Unfortunately, we cannot follow the harmonistic statement *bonum diffusivum sui*, which means that freedom conveys, as it were, its own quality of goodness. We must look into several features of freedom in order to warrant the suggestion that thematically and positionally it is indeed a good.

In the first place we must recall that freedom connotes a total stage or position and that particular or scattered acts are directed

---

4. Leibnitz: *Principles of Nature and Grace*, included in *The Monadology and other Philosophical Writings*, translated with introduction and notes by Robert Latta, Oxford University Press, London; Geoffrey Comberlege, 1945, p. 415.

towards their totalization, i.e. towards freedom. The very notion of totalization implies the aspect of aspiring at or striving for something. Freedom is an 'ought' and we are striving to achieve or realize it by reaching through totalization the position connoted by freedom. Freedom as a totality gives rise to the process of totalization and thus becomes an 'ought' for our aspirations. Let us recall in this context that the notion of 'ought' is etymologically cognate to the notion of 'owe' that is to say we 'owe' to do it. The same applies to the affinity of the German *das Sollen* with *die Schuld*, that is to say that we are *obliged* to direct ourselves towards freedom as a totality. Freedom as totality is never present — it is only a goal. At this juncture we should recall that in terms of the history of philosophical terms the term 'ought' or *das Sollen* emerged rather late, and in a way replaces the traditional term 'perfection'. Indeed it can be said that freedom as totality is a perfection of our acts of initiations, of decision, of directing a course of events. As the ego is understood as a total performer of acts of cognition, perception, etc., so freedom is the background and the total performer of the acts of initiation and decision. Thus it can be understood as the perfect stage of initiation, totalizing the scattered acts and providing the ground for their re-emergence in the situations to come. At this point the positional aspect of the 'ought' and the thematic aspect of the good are brought together — as indeed they are initially merged in the notion of perfection. Once the bifurcation between the thematic and the positional aspects is formulated, it becomes difficult to decide theoretically whether we should start our deduction from the positional aspect of the 'ought' or from the thematic aspect of the good. But be the root of our deduction what it may, eventually the two aspects coalesce in the notion of freedom. In any case we cannot take freedom to be a primary fact of reason, as Kant assumed it to be, but rather as a totalization and an interpretation of our acts, transferring the concept of freedom from being the underlying ground of our acts to being their ultimate focal point. In this sense the aspiration toward freedom implies the continuous attitude of affirmation and justification in the sense that we justify our particular and scattered decisions by referring them to their basis which, by the same token, is their *telos*. Our acts of decision are manifestations of freedom, though the total and manifested freedom is never present with us. Freedom calls for its realization, and it is established by acts of realization. In this sense the particular acts manifest freedom on the one hand and bring it about on the other. A present freedom would be a contradiction in terms because it would connote that freedom can be a fact and not only a focus of realization.

Since freedom is the focus of totalization, and is thus never completely established, it requires continuous protection. This aspect is translated as the right to be free. This in turn means the acknowledgement that freedom has to be safeguarded since it does not operate automatically. We sometimes translate that positional aspect of freedom as independence, as privacy in the individual context *vis-à-vis* other individuals and *vis-à-vis* society, but also in collective contexts, when we transpose the notion of freedom from the original individual sphere to collective entities, such as societies or states. But once we bring about that shift, we impose on the collective orbit the logic, as it were, of moral considerations, namely, we posit the collective entities in contexts of mutuality and reciprocity, i.e. one state versus another state. By the same token we impose the rhythm of the moral sphere on the collective entities, namely the distinction between particular acts and totality. The independence of the state is to be interpreted both as ground and as background for individual acts and decisions, but concurrently also as the sum-total of those acts, which contribute to the ever-increasing totalization of freedom *qua* independence.

At this juncture we again encounter the dilemma of the moral sphere. Freedom, as expressed in scattered acts or decisions but also in its total quality leads us to raise the question of the material meaning of these acts of decision and initiation, and their all-embracing quality merging in total freedom. Can we limit ourselves to the aspect of initiation and decision, disregarding the direction of our acts? It is obvious that the consideration in terms of reciprocity already imposes a sort of direction and even limitation on our decisions in their pure quality. But our concern with reciprocal contexts cannot be limited to the mere position of many individuals and the reciprocity which is brought about by the facticity of their co-presence. Should we rely, and this is one of the ways of rendering the question before us, exclusively on the spontaneity of the actor, and only *post factum* look into the consequences of that spontaneity, that is to say, find out after the event whether harm has been done to the other individual in the short run or in the long range; or should we take pre-emptive or preventive steps in order to safeguard the channels of spontaneity, and thus see freedom in its total *Gestalt*, i.e. as a spontaneity comprising the intentions as well as the direction of our acts and deeds? Kant, as well known, took the harmonistic and optimistic view that freedom takes care of itself, that is to say, that freedom, properly understood, by definition opts for universality, and thus for applicability *vis-à-vis* every human individual. In Kant's eyes freedom is therefore not only spontaneity and not only a totalization but constitutes its own synthesis between the decision and the direction to be followed or that which ought to be followed. Yet we cannot always maintain freedom both as a norm representing the focus of totalization and as a norm following the principle of universality or applicability to all individuals. Or perhaps we may put it thus in everyday language: empirically we cannot wait until freedom as perfection establishes itself. Therefore, acts of intervention and guidance are not only prudentially warranted but also morally legitimate, because the norm of reciprocity has obligations and demands of its own; it can even clash with the aspiration towards freedom and with the acts which allegedly express and manifest the total freedom to be established. At this point we come again to the notion of taking empirical considerations into account and taking them seriously — certainly more seriously than Kant, who relied on the invisible divine hand of humanity manifesting itself in freedom and its kingdom of harmony, to which it gives rise or birth. Hence we are led to an additional consideration pertaining to the moral sphere, which refers to the human condition here and now in the empirical world, and not only to perfectibility and perfection, which are, as we have seen, related to freedom as the total projection of individual acts of spontaneity or initiation.[5] We now turn to the next step of our analysis.

5. In a previous analysis the present author dealt, in a different context, with the 'ambiguity of the ethical situation'. See *Humanism in the Contemporary Era*, Mouton, The Hague, 1963, pp. 87ff.

(11)

Our analysis of the moral sphere and of the activity pertaining to it started out from the context of reciprocity. The shift towards freedom is an isolation of the agent from the context, in order to come back and to re-establish him within the context as a free actor, both in the sense of initiating deeds, giving them directions, taking upon himself the responsibility for his deeds and, last not least, maintaining himself as a total actor. It should be said that what is due to reciprocity is in fact due to it and we must take reciprocity seriously as a given and, at least to some extent, empirical context. Involvement in reciprocity can be interpreted as participation in the human world and therefore, in the context delineated by human partners. But that context is not only one between partners as objects or carriers of relations. Within the context of reciprocity the partners participate in particular modes of relation, like attraction, hatred, rejection and benevolence. They participate not only in attitudes and what emanates from them, but also in creations emerging in the human context — creations which in a sense can be termed goods, or modes of the good — and that term is not accidentally introduced here, since we are concerned with what is by definition the aspect of good. We can therefore say that certain creations, insofar as they reinforce reciprocity or correspond to the expectations of the actors, are goods. They can be material goods, like food or cloth, and they can be services, like medical care or educational facilities. The attribute of good can be conceived within the inter-human context as meeting the needs and expectations of the human beings involved, as well as opening the context for the realization of certain human expectations in the empirical world. To respond to the notion of the good or to that of the 'ought' in the empirical world is to open that world to the human individuals' share in it, either because that world is present and we acknowledge the human claim to have a share in the present world — and this in turn is one of the manifestations of openness — or because we recognize that meeting human needs and expectations is essential to reinforce the position of freedom. In this sense it can be said briefly — and trivially — that one has to live in order to be free, and to live is both an independent level of reality and an instrumental means for safeguarding free acts, and even more so, the projected or totalized version of freedom.

It is essential to remark here, and not out of historical considerations, that we are bound to take exception to the Kantian view of morality which stressed freedom only, disregarding the basic significance of material or empirical existence, and together with it the significance of empirical goods and our share in them. Insofar as one of the manifestations of the position of 'ought' is the position of a claim, in the sense that the 'ought' directs its claim towards the actors, the actors have a claim, which is basically directed towards the empirical realm of existence and not — or not only — towards the ontological or projectional status of freedom. Man can claim freedom, but freedom is silent or even mute in terms of its reference to the human actors. The human actor can demand freedom for himself because he has a certain conception of his position in the universe, that is to say, he gives a certain interpretation to his scattered acts. The empirical human being, participating in the empirical world, claims freedom for himself but his claim cannot be limited to freedom only. It is a claim directed at the empirical world in the sense of making that world open to him, enabling him to make this claim and accepting it as meant to establish and reinforce human existence in the given context. We thus encounter here the two levels of the moral sphere: the totalizing level of freedom and the level of particularity in terms of the goods available or about to be available to empirical human beings. The moral perspective turns, that is interprets, the encounter between human beings and the given world into an encounter between opportunities and services and the concrete human being. To put it differently, the moral perspective removes the encounter from the merely factual level and justifies that encounter by turning the surrounding world into a sum-total of opportunities or materials to be placed at the disposal of human beings. From the moral perspective, the empirical human being indeed becomes a citizen of two worlds, of the empirical goods as well of the trans-empirical freedom. The empirical human being establishes the bridge between those two worlds by claiming for himself the right to participate in the given goods, and by claiming for himself also the focus of freedom which reinforces his position in the world, including his position as a claiming or demanding entity. The moral perspective justifies the position of claimant in both directions, or, in other words, the inclination and the urge are turned into justified claims through and by virtue — in the strict sense — of the moral perspective. To be sure, that turn is more visible *vis-à-vis* the empirical world than *vis-à-vis* freedom. It would be somewhat far-fetched to speak about the urge to be free, since the totalization implied in freedom is certainly more of an interpreted character than it is a shift from needs to claims.

Commenting again on Kant's approach to morality, we come back to an issue we have already dealt with, namely that of common humanity, which, as we have seen, appears in Kant as providing the justification for treating human beings not only as means but also as ends. It seems more appropriate to introduce the notion of common humanity in terms of what we can describe as the participational aspect of morality than in terms of the ontological position of individuals or their freedom. The world of humanity is, at least partially, a world of reciprocity. Each one of us has his share in that world — a visible or an invisible one. The presence of human beings is a presence of a continuous activity, whether that activity be explicit or implicit, whether it has distinct results or whether those results are immersed in the anonymous course of events. The presence of every human being in the inter-human context, i.e. in humanity as a sum-total of human acts and performances, and not only as human potentiality, creates the background for the particular moral perspective which bases the right of human beings to participate in the context of humanity upon their presence in that very context. Because of this consideration we see that the moral perspective introduces the notion of rights, that is, of justified claims, into the universe of human activities. Since there exists the primary involvement in the world of humanity as well as the shift from the involvement to its affirmation via the notion of rights, we realize that moral perspective becomes, or can become, interlaced with the political sphere. The political sphere is a primary one in terms of human coexistence. Moral perspective superimposes its own concepts or, as we call them, norms, i.e.

yardsticks of evaluation and pursuit, on the political context, Moral perspective initiates the demands *vis-à-vis* the given coexistence, or evokes a sense of participation in it, thus turning the given context of coexistence into an open context, open to human deeds, aspirations, evaluations and ideas.

It is again in this sense that we realize the meta-character of moral perspective, which expresses itself — among other expressions — in combining the political aspect of coexistence with the moral aspect of openness. This meta-character becomes prominent when we observe the overlapping of the activity of working and the exchangeability of goods with moral perspective, in two senses: (a) the perspective of openness as introduced into the inter-human contact or intercourse on the level of exchangeability — for instance when we refer to honest wages of honest trade — thus introducing a moral norm into an activity whose initial *raison d'être* does not lie in moral considerations or intentions; (b) when out of moral considerations we turn the political context into an agency providing for human aspirations or needs by creating work or opening opportunities for mobility through work, or by rendering services of different sorts. However, *mutantis mutandis* the meta-character of the moral sphere is visible also *vis-à-vis* the activity of play, though that activity has its own rules, and is thus a sort of enclave, as we have seen in our previous analysis. The openness is not only another aspect of the encounter between partners in a claim, but, for instance, carries with it the meaning and the imperative of honesty, of refraining from cheating, being a 'good loser', etc. It is again plausible to assume that the meta-character of moral perspective takes the shape of an intervening activity *vis-à-vis* the intervening activity of labour and work, more so than *vis-à-vis* the semi-secluded character of play, in spite of the fact that the moral activity is visible, as is the play. But once roles are prescribed, the aspect of attitudes or intentions — again in the Kantian sense of *Gesinnung* — is less significant than when 'serious' acts are performed. Attitudes and intentions are viewed as constant factors in the human position and are thus taken as anchors for human behaviour in terms of day-to-day acts on the one hand and moral attitudes on the other.

It is indeed at this point that we have to look into additional aspects of the meeting between the trans-empirical level of morality, focused around freedom, and the empirical level, related to the notion of sharing and participating. The significance attributed in moral discussions to the notion of character and to the notion of virtues is a case in point. Character connotes a total constant attitude, virtues connote partial attitudes in certain directions, like truthfulness, faithfulness, bravery, etc. In both notions — character and virtues — the emphasis is placed on constancy, that is to say that human beings will initiate acts guided by a certain pattern or, from a different angle, their acts will be grounded in certain convictions which have infiltrated the psyche to such an extent that they have become constant guiding factors. The notion of character and virtues is one that serves as a bridge between the constant norm in the thematic sense and the individual as he stands here and now in the empirical sense. Here, too, we cannot conceive of the notion of character and virtues outside the architectonic position of morality, as placed between the trans-empirical and empirical, and not exclusively immersed in the trans-empirical, as Kant had it. As a matter of fact, Kant himself could not escape this — let us call it — respect for the empirical, as we see in his philosphy of education and virtues.[6]

(12)

Coming back to the aspect of intention as characteristic of the moral sphere, and as presupposed by and implied in, the moral activity, we can conclude by saying that it is part of the moral norm to be obeyed out of conviction or out of intention. Here we follow the Kantian line in general as well as the suggestion made by Kant about the difference between morality and legality, namely that legality connotes a conduct in accordance with the law, while morality connotes a conduct in accordance with the imperative or arising from the intention corresponding to acknowledgement of the validity of the principle. Yet it is

6. See John R. Silber: 'Human Action and the Language of Volitions', *Proceedings of the Aristotelian Society*, Vol LXIV, 1964, pp. 199ff.

essential to comment on the relationship between morality and the legal system even without pretending to exhaust the issue. The comment we shall make is meant only to reinforce the exploration of morality and its actions.

The affinity between the legal system and morality is obvious in that both connote codes of conduct or norms. Having already mentioned the Kantian juxtaposition, we must point out additional features which emphasize the difference between legality and morality. To put that difference in the context of our discussion, it has to be said that the legal system refers mainly to the order or the coexistence between human beings, and thus to the political sphere, whilst morality refers in the first place to reciprocity. Reciprocity connotes not only the co-presence of individuals but relations developing and emerging between them. What Moritz Schlick[7] said about laws of nature, that they are abbreviated expressions of order (*abgekürzte Ausdrücke der Ordnung*) applies, *mutatis mutandis*, to the legal system in the human context, that is to say, that it is an abbreviated formulation of order. Though it is now part of everyday vernacular to speak of law and order in the same breath, this conjunction is to extent tautological because law refers to order and is meant to reinforce it. It is because of this inherent relationsip to order that the legal system can eventually be endowed with the qualities of enactment or enforcement, because state institutions, representing the primary order and meant to reinforce it, use the legal system as agency or instrument and add to it the force of compulsion. Since the emphasis lies on the aspect of order, we can speak of good and bad laws, because laws are meant in the first place to provide order or to add to it. Thus they are meant to be primarily instrumental and gauged from that point of view, and not good in the sense of openness, as we tried to investigate in the preceding part of our analysis. Since we move, or perhaps are placed from the very beginning, in the scope of coexistence, we speak of the purpose of law in terms of the common or public interest, though in terms of justice we em-

7. M. Schlick: 'Kausalität im täglichen Leben und in der Wissenschaft', included in *Erkenntnisprobleme der Naturwissenschaften*, herausgegeben von L. Krüger, Köln/ Berlin, 1970, p. 143.

phasize the affinity between the legal system and morality, because justice, at least in its distributive direction, has the quality of openness which we identified as an essential characteristic of morality. In any case, morality is meant to be good by definition and not only partly so, and bad morality would be a contradiction in terms — but bad laws are not. Morality lacks enforcement precisely because it refers to convictions or intentions, and, as we put it before, these belong to the very substance of the norm. There is indeed an overlap between morality and legality. Once we are aware of the difference in points of departure, namely reciprocity as distinct from coexistence, we notice that morality is a sphere more loaded than legality, that is to say, it involves more demands and claims than the system of laws. The overlap is there because we can interpret, and rightly so, reciprocity as presupposing coexistence and thus as being an elaboration or a manifestation of the primary coexistence. Hence it follows that legality is in a sense more basic than morality. However, this is not meant as a statement in terms of the chronological sequence referring to the primacy of legality over morality, but to the descriptive character of the two spheres. The minimum component (laws) versus the maximum component (principles) is visible also in the fact that only certain modes of behaviour can be prescribed by legality, but a greater number can or ought to be described by morality. Legality can prescribe refraining from infringement or encroaching on the domain of the other person, but it cannot prescribe a benevolent attitude or respect or, as we may put it, going out of one's way for the sake of the other person. The latter is rather an elaboration or nuance of reciprocity, and thus belongs to the moral sphere proper.

(13)

A comment should be made here on the topic of the relation between morality and religion, keeping in mind the inherent complexity of the subject. Some remarks however are called for, because the mode of affinity between morality and religion differs from that between morality and legality. While legality, as we have seen, is not grounded in convictions, or, to use a softer term, in attitudes, religion refers to attitudes or evokes them. The attitude of piety, of acceptance, or even awareness of one's place in the universe is essential for religion. Let us put it somewhat differently: religions not evoking attitudes cease to be living religions and become confined to scriptures or to documents, while the scriptures and the documents make primarily manifest not only dogmas but also modes of adherence to them. Once we place the emphasis on the aspect of attitudes, we can move one step further in identifying the affinity between religions and morality by saying that religions evoke a certain conduct and not only one of prayer and worship but of involvement between human beings. Yet precisely at this point, even when we attribute norms of conduct to religions, we have to ask the question to what extent do religions, out of their own logic, presuppose human reciprocity as a primary fact or dimension, or whether they presuppose rather the attitudes of men *vis-à-vis* the divine realm as a primary direction and dimension. Out of that awareness human reciprocity can emerge and can become open to the normative guidance of commandments or prescriptions. But the point of departure is, for instance, the awareness of human finitude or of the position of man as created in the image of God, and not human reciprocity as given and calling for a continuous reinforcement and re-shaping. If this is so, then the presence of attitudes or convictions characteristic of both religion and morality cannot obscure the substantive aspect of the former, that is to say, that morality in the first place has an inter-human connotation, while religion is in the first place meant to establish *religio*, i.e. the relationship between man and the divine realm; the inter-human dimension is a consequence and not a presupposition. This applies also – and especially – to religions imbued with a fundamental ethical content, like the biblical religions.

But at this juncture a second comment is apposite, which refers to the second pole of morality, i.e. the position of the norms. We have seen the basic importance of freedom in moral considerations. Freedom is, as we have attempted to elucidate, trans-factual or trans-empirical. But in that position freedom does not call for a new ontological level above the empirical one – above and still on an ontological level. The emphasis we placed on totalization was meant to emphasize precisely this aspect, namely that freedom is related to empirical conduct and acts, and goes beyond them without ever overstepping them by placing itself in a new ontological order. In this sense morality relies on convictions responding to norms, without grounding the norms ontologically. Not only does the human being occupy an in-between position between the empirical and trans-empirical — but the norms, too, occupy an in-between position between the ontological and let us call it the para-ontological level. The latter would here connote the dependence of the norm on interpretations, on progressing towards totalization without reaching totality.

The characteristic feature of religions in terms of their structural logic is that religions anchor norms ontologically. They relate the norm to the divine realm or consider the two identical — and this logic applies to religions in their different modes, let us say both the Brahmanism and to the biblical religions. If one were to take a critical view, one could say that religions imply a projection of norms onto the ontological realm. But if one were to make only a descriptive analysis, one could say that religion is based on conviction, that a self-supporting morality, referring to the polarity of norms and convictions, cannot perform its function and needs a grounding in an ontological dimension or stratum of or in the universe. It is not by chance therefore that religions cannot take freedom as a basic norm, precisely because of the very dependence of the world and of human beings on the trans-empirical ontological stratum which is the divine existence. Moreover, religions sometimes struggle with the issue of freedom, not only when they are inclined in the direction of predetermination of human acts, but even when they allow for the paradox or the tension expressed in the Talmudic saying: 'Everything is foreseen, and the choice is given.' The exploration of the nature of morality cannot serve as an anti-religious argument, because such an exploration would have to refer to the self-enclosed character of morality and to an attempt to describe it within that enclosure. Religion by its very essence opens up the self-enclosure and therefore presents a metaphysical or ontological grounding for morality. Perhaps we should here make a distinction between a metaphysical approach and an ontological one: a metaphysical approach proposes to analyze morality on its own terms by attempting to identify the point of departure of morality in the given world, i.e. in inter-human reciprocity. The ontological approach, which at this point replaces the phenomenological approach, may accept several aspects or even conclusions of such an exploration but will transpose them from the reference to the given world to the dependence upon the transempirical ontologically warranted reality. At this point the religious interest may take advantage of the philosophical exploration of morality but it has its own logic and thrust. A philosophical exposition may deal with the structure of religion or religions with the understanding that the religions go beyond the data to which the phenomenologically shaped philosophical approach is primarily related.

(14)

The particular quality of the moral activity came to the fore in the previous analysis because of the singular interrelation between that activity and the content which bestows on it its specific quality, *qua* moral. The activity is performed by empirical human beings. These beings overstep the boundaries of the empirical realm by the trend toward totalization, by the relation to freedom as a factor of determination not detached from determination by the surrounding environment but also by the position of the 'I' as a free totality within the boundaries of singularity. This interaction does not obviate the aspect of belonging to the empirical realm which is characteristic of the activity as activity. Hence the question of the determination of the moral activity in its relation to the norm or norms emerges in the sphere. It is that aspect which is expressed in the problem of the relativity of moral norms to which we referred briefly in a previous part of our discussion.

The religious interpretation of morality which implies the grounding of norms in the divine entity, thus interpreting them as divine prescriptions, is obviously an attempt to overcome a possible relativistic interpretation. Since the divine entity is not an empirical entity, it may follow that whatever stems from it as a norm appears to be a divine commandment. Thus the removal of the norms from the empirical sphere also denies the possible approach of looking at them as grounded in empirical situations. The relativistic interpretation of morality is thus precluded by definition, or if we may use such an expression, by the very topography of the moral realm.

Yet a closer look at the position of the norms within the scope of a religious interpretation raises some sceptical questions as to the validity of this attempt. We may discern a parallel between the ethical norm and the principles of logic: does God prescribe the norm because it is intrinsically good or does it become good because God prescribes it? Similarly in terms of cognitive principles: are they binding because God has posited them, or has God accepted them because they are inescapably logical or cognitive principles?

In this sceptical attitude to the religious interpretation — in spite of the impact it has had and still has on the interpretation of morality and the continued attempt to safeguard the positions of the norms *vis-à-vis* the ethical situation — we find an additional justification for establishing the semi-independence of the moral sphere by emphasizing the phenomenological approach to it.

(15)

The presence of the empirical component or stratum within the scope of morality is obvious. The human beings involved in the context of co-existence and in the structure of mutuality are not created by the moral activity and the various modes of it. Their existence within the moral sphere is taken for granted by the activity within that sphere and by the norm guiding it. *Primum vivere* applies here not to the move to philosophy but also to the moral interpretation of the *vivere*. The moral interpretation represents a leap as compared with the acknowledgement of the presence of human beings inherent in mutuality as such, let alone in exchanges taking place against its background.

Let us here interpose a comment bearing on the presence of the given stratum in terms of the norms intended to guide it or to guide behaviour inside it. To take as a paradigm the creation of the empirical stratum by God, who is guided by his adherence to the idea of the good: once the world is created it proceeds according to its course and has its own structure. The goodness bringing about the presence does not make the presence continuously dependent on the idea, even when an occasionalistic interpretation of the dependence of human knowledge on God is brought into the context. The empirical stratum is present even when we introduce a genetic or what is called creationist interpretation of that presence. This argument holds good *a fortiori* within the boundaries of an emprical acknowledgement of the given facts: they are there, and the moral activity and the norm or norms related to the empirical human existence amount to an interpretation of the given acts and not to an emanation of them. The presence, we are suggesting, seems to be the possible anchor of any relativistic interpretation of morality. The existing stratum becomes a situation: anthropological, cultural, historical, psychological and so on, and guides the moral activity and its norms. The ontological or existential dependence on the given becomes a thematic dependence on it.

Here seems to lie the leap characteristic of a relativistic interpretation. An interpretation inherent in the moral activity is expressed in the move from accepting the mutuality of human beings leading to the recognition of every human being in his own status. It is an interpretation needing mutuality as a *conditio sine que non*, but as such it cannot be explained by that *sine qua non*. It is an interpretation expressing a reflection on the position of human beings, and the very fact that a value status is attributed to every human being is a step beyond or above the empirically given data. The recognition of the positions of every human being implies the interpretation of that position in terms of the individual involved. Thus it is a sort of a separation of the individual from the context or lifting him above it. From the perspective of the interpretation of the individual, an interpretation underlying recognition, the status of an 'I' is attributed to the individual and the motivation of freedom is assigned to him. These are interpretations which by the same token are turned into norms and as such their universe of discourse ceases to be the empirical stratum and becomes the moral context. The activity is manifested in terms of the norm while the norm refers to the position of the 'I' and his freedom, although it is clear that the activity and the norm represent a circle which is both self-enclosed and open to the empirical situation.

(16)

One of the important manifestations of this dependence on the empirical stratum on the one hand and the lack of dependence on it on the other is the fact that the level of materialization of the norms is the empirical one: recognition of the human being is meant to be manifested in terms of the factual human beings empirically encountered. This position is exemplified in the realization of the position of freedom. Freedom is not a sort of an outward ideal. It is meant to guide the actions of human beings, as well as to reserve a refuge of privacy, to safeguard freedom of expression, and so on. These norms are broad, but their realization is piecemeal because of the essence of empirical existence and the human beings involved in it. The surplus of the norm, to call it that, is both its strength and its weakness because it does not enable it to be totally realized in the empirical context. Yet the piecemeal character of this realization means that the norm is related to empirical circumstances but not dependent upon them, as the relativistic interpretation tends to have it.[8]

In terms of the relation between reflection and action the following remarks may wind up our discussion. The moral activity and the norms to which it is related presuppose the perspective of interpretation even more than do the other modes of activity we have already discussed, though there is of course no mode of activity free from interpretation. The more 'abstract' the mode of activity is, the more it is grounded in interpretation. Yet no

8. There is a vast literature dealing with ethical relativism. Part of that literature is mentioned in two articles by the present author: 'On Ethical Relativism', *Journal of Value Inquiry*, Vol. XI, 1977, pp. 81ff; and 'Relativity and Relativism', in *Albert Einstein, Historical and Cultural Perspectives, The Centennial Symposium in Jerusalem*, ed. Gerald Holton and Yehuda Elkana, Princeton University Press, Princeton, 1982, pp. 175ff.

interpretation which is related to action can disregard action. This is so not only because of our involvement in action but because one of the foci of interpretation is to guide action. Thus in order to fulfil the 'logic' of interpretation it is mandatory to come back to action. Within the moral scope the attempt to cling to interpretation only would amount to 'words, words' and this in a sense would defy the meaning and the locus of morality.

INDEX OF NAMES

INDEX OF SUBJECTS